The
FCPA
in **Latin America**

*Common Corruption Risks and Effective
Compliance Strategies for the Region*

Matteson Ellis

A Corporate Compliance Insights Publication

© Matteson Ellis 2016

Print ISBN: 978-0-69276-452-7

eBook ISBN: 978-1-48357-690-9

Table of Contents

ACKNOWLEDGEMENTS xi

FOREWORD xv

Referenced FCPA Cases xix

CHAPTER 1

Introduction: Latin American Compliance Bridges 1

Misconception #1: "Isn't corruption just part of Latin American culture?" ... 14

Misconception #2: "Isn't the FCPA bad for business?" 17

Misconception #3: "The FCPA wrongly targets foreigners; you have corruption in the United States, too." 19

Misconception #4: "The FCPA is misguided; you can't end corruption in Latin America." 21

CHAPTER 2

Latin America: A Melting Pot of Corruption Risks 23

Public Procurement Manipulation 26

Regulatory Risks 30

Risks at Customs 33

Police and Extortion 36

Facilitating Payments 42

Family-Owned Businesses and Acquisitions 45

Monopolies and Compliance Risk 47

Risks When Bubbles Burst 50

CHAPTER 3

Specific Corruption Risks in Key Latin American Markets 55

Argentina: Corruption Risks on the Río de la Plata 56

Brazil: A Time of Dramatic Anti-Corruption Developments 59

Chile: Understanding Local Law, Enforcement, and Deterrence 63

Colombia: Legacy Risks During A Quiet Boom 66

Mexico: Corruption in a Familiar Market..70

Peru: The Shadow of Fujimori...73

Venezuela: Corruption Risk in Political and Economic Chaos....................76

CHAPTER 4

Conveying Anti-Corruption Compliance to Latin American Business Leaders..81

Setting the Stage... 82

Describing the FCPA's Anti-Bribery Provisions............................. 85

Emphasizing the FCPA's Accounting Provisi 86

Highlighting the Riskiness of Bribery... 94

Explaining Declinations and the Meaning of "Rogue Employee"............... 96

Demonstrating How FCPA Compliance Is Good For The Bottom Line....... 99

CHAPTER 5

Tailored Compliance Strategies for Companies in Latin America............103

The Importance of Risk-Based Programs in Latin America.......................104

Targeting Compliance Training to Latin American Employees...................108

Avoiding Sham Contracts and Phantom Vendors....................................114

Monitoring as a Sign of a Mature Compliance Program 121

How Small- and Medium-Sized Enterprises Meet Compliance Expectations 124

When to Use Outside Help for FCPA Compliance Matters.......................128

CHAPTER 6

Where Culture Fits Into Compliance in Latin America 131

The "Circle of Trust" in Compliance..132

Focusing on Values 136

Appealing to Emotion 140

Cultural Nuances in Internal Reporting Mechanisms...............................142

CHAPTER 7

Managing Third-Party Relationships in Latin America 147

Mitigating Third-Party Risk 151

Determining the Scope of Third-Party Due Diligence 155

Common Third-Party Red Flags 160

Responding to Third-Party Pushback 165

Handling Third-Party Due Diligence Backlogs 168

Transferring Third-Party Due Diligence to Business Units 171

Managing Third Parties Related To Government Officials 173

Responding in the Face of Third-Party Corruption 177

CHAPTER 8

FCPA Enforcement in Latin America: Caught in the Web 181

The Broad Reach of the FCPA into Latin America 182

How FCPA Enforcement Officials Discover Violations 186

The Importance of Internal FCPA Investigations 189

When to Use Outside Counsel for FCPA Investigations 194

Knowing When to Voluntarily Disclose 196

Why FCPA Investigations Are Costly 200

Minimizing Internal Investigation Costs 203

Establishing Credibility with FCPA Enforcement Officials 206

Index 211

Disclaimer

The information in the book is intended for public discussion and educational purposes only. It is not intended to provide legal advice or an opinion on specific facts to the book's readers, and does not create an attorney-client relationship. It does not seek to describe or convey the quality of any legal services.

The book's author encourages readers to seek qualified legal counsel regarding the U.S. Foreign Corrupt Practices Act, anti-corruption laws or any other legal issue.

The passages of this book reflect the views of the author in his individual capacity, and do not necessarily represent the views of anyone else, including the entities with which the author is affiliated and the author's employer.

Neither the author nor anyone with whom the author is affiliated shall be responsible for any losses incurred by a reader or a company as a result of information provided in this book. Neither the author nor anyone with whom the author is affiliated makes any warranties, representations, or claims of any kind about such information. For example, the information contained here may not be up-to-date, may not reflect the most current laws or changes in the law, or may not apply to your individual circumstances. These materials should in no way be read as an indication of future results.

For more information about these issues, please contact the author. The invitation to contact the author is not to be construed as a solicitation for legal work. Any new lawyer-client relationship will be confirmed in writing.

ACKNOWLEDGEMENTS

This book, the first of its kind to focus on the U.S. Foreign Corruption Practices Act ("FCPA") in Latin America, is the result of a collective effort of several individuals, spanning various countries, cultures, professions, and sectors, each person with an interest in international anti-corruption issues. In particular, the book's content is inspired by discussions and debates I have had over the years with people from three different groups.

The Anti-Corruption Mafia: In the mid-2000s, when U.S. government officials were beginning to enforce the FCPA with great vigor, a group of young professionals in Washington DC formed what we dubbed the "Anti-Corruption Mafia". We were lawyers, accountants, investigators, and policymakers, all still junior in our professions and all connected in some way to the developing world of anti-corruption compliance and enforcement. The Anti-Corruption Mafia dreamed big about the day when the FCPA would be a household name in international business, anti-corruption laws would be taken seriously in regions known for endemic corruption risk, companies in far-flung corners of the globe would ask how corporate compliance works, people in pivotal jurisdictions would take to the streets to demand that governm   representatives be held accountable for unethical and self-serving actions, and countries that had signed on to international anti-corruption treaties would actually adopt and enforce the laws they promised.

The core members of the Mafia were Matthew Fowler, Aneta and Greg Wierzynski, David Wolfe, Jamieson Smith, Lina Braude, and Lynn Robitaille. Since that time, they have each gone on to assume impressive roles as directors, partners, compliance officers, adjudicators, and investigators at esteemed institutions as diverse as The World Bank, the Inter-American Development Bank, the Global Fund, a top law firm, a Fortune 200 company, and a forensic science commission. Others who influenced the Mafia's work along the way included Noah Bopp of The School for Ethics and Global Leadership and my former colleagues from The World Bank's Integrity Vice Presidency, like Mazhar Inayat, Nodir Zakirov, and Patrick Kelkar. Congrats to the Anti-Corruption Mafia – our dreams appear to be coming true.

The Blogosphere. Many of the thoughts in this book come from five years of writing about anti-corruption matters in Latin America on the FCPAméricas Blog. Along the way, my "blog compatriot" has been Carlos Ayres, Brazil's preeminent anti-corruption attorney. Carlos and I always envisioned the blog as a tool to help educate Latin America on the nature and importance of anti-corruption enforcement and compliance developments – in English, Spanish, and Portuguese. Others along the way have given life and color to the blog, like Matthew Fowler, Mila Grandes, and dozens of contributors. The blog never would have started had it not been for the encouragement of the prolific Tom Fox over a Starbucks coffee that fateful day in 2011. Tom's guidance along the way has been indispensable.

The Firm: In an age where law firm loyalty is rare, I chose to return to Miller & Chevalier after a solo law firm stint for a good reason. Few Washington DC firms with international reach offer Miller & Chevalier's mix of congeniality, teamwork, and substance. I have had the great honor to cut my teeth under the "Dean" of the FCPA Bar, Homer E. Moyer, Jr., who graciously agreed to write this book's Foreword. Other firm superstars, like Kate Atkinson, Mark Rochon, and James Tillen, regularly take me under their wings, together navigating complex issues in a narrow field of law, for which I am grateful. It took a lot to finish this book, and it would not have happened without Miller & Chevalier colleagues, including Mary Lou Soller and others.

This book is the result of years of professional collaboration with these individuals, all of whom share a common trait, which drives our work in the field of anti-corruption law and policy. It is a trait that is commonplace in Latin America and provides fuel to the following chapters...*passion*.

FOREWORD

The FCPA in Latin America

Often overlooked in the fast-moving, ever-expanding world of anti-corruption law is the fact that the first international anti-corruption convention was neither the Organization for Economic Co-operation and Development ("OECD") convention, widely regarded as the most successful of all the conventions, nor the comprehensive United Nations Convention against Corruption ("UNCAC"), which was, in fact, the last such convention to be negotiated. Rather, the first was the Inter-American Convention against Corruption ("the OAS convention"), concluded in Caracas on March 29, 1996, some 20 months before member states of the OECD reached agreement on the OECD's "Convention on Combatting Bribery of Foreign Public Officials in International Business Transactions," more digestibly known as the "OECD Anti-Bribery Convention."

It is thus fair to say that it was the countries of Latin America, along with their neighbors to the north, that first committed in principle to a strong, multi-lateral anti-corruption convention. And the OAS convention remains notable for covering the acceptance, as well as the payment, of bribes, illicit enrichment of officials, mutual cooperation, and recovery and repatriation of the proceeds of bribery. As a result, in Latin America the legal architecture of anti-bribery law is well-established, as virtually every country in South America has signed and ratified this convention.

Committing in principle and signing a convention are different, however, from effectively implementing and enforcing its provisions. That observation, which is applicable to every convention that has been concluded, continues to be a problem for even the OECD convention, the most sophisticated of all. Even in those countries in which enforcement is most active, including the United States, consistent, active enforcement did not follow immediately upon enactment of anti-bribery laws. Rather, enforcement has typically come gradually, with broad public awareness of bribery prohibitions lagging even further behind visible enforcement.

As with many regions of the world, awareness of the legal superstructure of anti-bribery law came first through the aggressive extraterritorial application of domestic laws, the U.S. Foreign Corrupt Practices Act ("FCPA"), in the first instance. As Chapter 1 of this book notes, the FCPA – which, like all domestic laws prohibiting bribery of foreign public officials, is inherently extraterritorial – has been applied to cases of bribery of officials in almost all of the countries of South America, and massive investigations are now being conducted under domestic laws of Latin American countries. As a consequence, we are now entering an era of what one UK lawyer long ago called "convention congestion," with the attendant complications of parallel, overlapping, and sometimes conflicting multi-jurisdictional investigations.

Against this backdrop, this book by Matteson Ellis is not just timely, but also an enormously valuable reference source filled with practical, usable advice and insights. Now a partner of mine at Miller & Chevalier, Matt brings to bear experience that he has gained, first, several years ago as a part of our own busy anti-corruption practice, followed by experience as an investigator for the Integrity Vice Presidency of the World Bank and then as a pioneer working on his own as anti-corruption law and practice in Latin America was rapidly expanding. As a result, Matt Ellis is uniquely qualified for the task he set for himself.

The pages that follow paint an accurate and informative picture of current enforcement patterns and the risks they present, particularly for major corporations. To concrete examples and real cases, he adds cultural insights that make this book relevant and eminently practical. The advice offered is borne of years of experience gained by Matt, together with a deep bench of colleagues who have also long been immersed in this critical area of the law.

Perhaps most important, however, are the chapters that discuss preventive measures. Companies aware of the risks of being caught in an anti-bribery investigation as a result of ignorance, neglect, or missteps of one or a few of its employees have a special interest in preventing problems, which is the focus of a substantial portion of this book. Companies have little trouble locating law firms that are eager to help, after-the-fact, in dealing with a likely violation, an internal investigation, or a government enforcement action. That category of legal work is labor-intensive, expensive, favored (as a result) by many firms, and potentially open-ended in scope.

The smarter money goes into effective, individually tailored, risk-based preventive measures which can, if effectively and sensitively designed and implemented, help create a culture of respect for and compliance with the law. In addition, an effective compliance program can enable companies to move quickly, ameliorate risks, minimize the diversion of company resources, and save money. Better still, they may help companies prevent issues and ambiguous situations from becoming violations at all and will, in any event, equip a company and its lawyers to deal with potential violations as promptly and cost-effectively as possible.

As you are the one who has paid for and now owns the book, you are, of course, free to read as much of it or as little as you wish. However, to get your money's worth – and much more – start at the beginning and read it straight through. Then keep it handy. And, since perfection is elusive, . . . *buena suerte!*

Homer E. Moyer, Jr.

Miller & Chevalier Chartered

Washington, DC

Referenced FCPA Cases

Case Name	SEC Case Citation	DOJ Case Citation
ABB Limited	SEC v. ABB, Ltd., No. 10-cv-1648 (D.D.C. Sept. 29, 2010)	United States v. ABB Inc., No. 10-cr-664 (S.D. Tex. Sept. 29, 2010)
Alcatel-Lucent Société Anonyme	SEC v. Alcatel-Lucent, S.A., No. 10-cv-24620 (S.D. Fla. Dec. 27, 2010)	United States v. Alcatel-Lucent, S.A., No. 10-cr-20907 (S.D. Fla. Dec. 27, 2010)
Christian Sapsizian (former Alcatel-Lucent Société Anonyme executive)		United States v. Sapsizian, No. 6-cr-20797 (S.D. Fla. Mar. 20, 2007)
Alcoa Incorporated	In the Matter of Alcoa Inc., Exchange Act Release No. 71261 (Jan. 9, 2014)	United States v. Alcoa World Alumina LLC, No. 14-cr-7 (W.D. Pa. Jan. 9, 2014)
Alstom Société Anonyme		United States v. Alstom S.A., 14-cr-246 (S.D.N.Y. Dec. 22, 2014)
American Rice Incorporated	SEC v. Murphy, et al., No. H-02-2908 (S.D. Tex. July 30, 2002)	United States v. Kay, No. 01-cr-914 (S.D. Tex. Oct. 6, 2004); United States v. Kay, 359 F.3d 738 (5th Cir. 2004)
Aon Corporation	SEC vs. Aon Corp., No. 11-cv-2256 (D.D.C. Dec. 20, 2011)	Non-Pros. Agreement, In re Aon Corp. (Dec. 20, 2011)
Avon Products Incorporated	SEC v. Avon Products Inc., No. 14-cv-9956 (S.D.N.Y. Dec. 17, 2014)	United States v. Avon Products, Inc., No. 14-cr-828 (S.D.N.Y. Dec. 17, 2014)
Baker Hughes Incorporated	In the Matter of Baker Hughes Inc., Exchange Act Release No. 44784 (Sept. 12, 2001); SEC v. Baker Hughes Inc., et al., No. 07-cv-1408 (S.D. Tex. Apr. 26, 2007)	United States v. Baker Hughes Svcs. Int'l, No. 07-cr-129 (S.D. Tex. Apr. 11, 2007)
Ball Corporation	In the Matter of Ball Corp., Exchange Act Release No. 64123 (Mar. 24, 2011)	
Banco de Desarollo Economico y Social de Venezuela		United States v. Clarke, et al., No. 13-cr-901 (S.D.N.Y. May 7, 2013)
BellSouth Corporation	SEC v. BellSouth Corp., No. 02-cv-113 (N.D. Ga. Jan. 15, 2002)	
Biomet Incorporated	SEC v. Biomet, Inc., No. 12-cv-454 (D.D.C. Mar. 26, 2012)	United States v. Biomet, Inc., No. 12-cr-80 (D.D.C. Mar. 26, 2012)
Bizjet International Sales and Support Incorporated		United States v. BizJet Int'l Sales and Support, Inc., No. 12-cr-61 (N.D. Okla. Mar. 14, 2012)

Case Name	SEC Case Citation	DOJ Case Citation
Bridgestone Corporation		United States v. Bridgestone Corp., No. 11-cr-651 (S.D. Tex. Sept. 15, 2011)
Dallas Airmotive Incorporated		United States v. Dallas Airmotive, Inc., No. 14-cr-483 (Dec. 10, 2014)
Diageo Public Limited Company	In re Diageo plc, Exchange Act Release No. 64978 (July 27, 2011)	
Direct Access Partners Limited Liability Company	SEC v. Clarke, et al., No. 13-cv-3074 (S.D.N.Y. May 7, 2013)	United States v. Clarke, et al., No. 13-cr-901 (S.D.N.Y. May 7, 2013)
Eli Lilly and Company	SEC v. Eli Lilly and Co., No. 12-cv-2045 (D.D.C. Dec. 20, 2012)	
Helmerich & Payne Incorporated	In the Matter of Helmerich & Payne, Inc., Exchange Act Release No. 60400 (July 30, 2009)	Non-Pros. Agreement, In re Helmerich & Payne, Inc. (July 29, 2009)
Hewlett-Packard Company	In the Matter of Hewlett-Packard Co., Exchange Act Release No. 71916 (Apr. 9, 2014)	Non-Pros. Agreement, In re Hewlett-Packard Mexico, S de R.L. de C.V. (Apr. 9, 2014); United States v. Hewlett-Packard Polska, SP. Z O.O., No. 14-cr-202 (N.D. Cal. Apr. 9, 2014); United States v. Zao Hewlett-Packard A.O., No. 14-cr-201 (N.D. Cal. Apr. 9, 2014)
LAN Airlines Sociedad Anónima	In the Matter of Ignacio Cueto Plaza, Exchange Act Release No. 77057 (Feb. 4, 2016)	
Morgan Stanley and Company Incorporated	SEC v. Peterson, No. 12-cv-2033 (E.D.N.Y. Apr. 25, 2012)	United States v. Peterson, No. 12-cr-224 (E.D.N.Y. Apr. 25, 2012)
Nature's Sunshine Products Incorporated	SEC v. Nature's Sunshine Products, Inc., et al., No. 09-cv-0672 (D. Utah, July 29, 2009)	
Orthofix International Naamloze Vennootschap	SEC v. Orthofix Int'l, N.V., No. 12-cv-419 (E.D. Tex. July 10, 2012)	United States v. Orthofix Int'l, N.V., No. 12-cr-150 (E.D. Tex. July 10, 2012)
Panalpina Incorporated	SEC v. Panalpina, Inc., No. 10-cv-4334 (S.D. Tex. Nov. 4, 2010)	United States v. Panalpina, Inc., No. 10-cr-765 (S.D. Tex. Nov. 4, 2010)
Paradigm Besloten Vennootschap		Non-Pros. Agreement, In re Paradigm B.V. (Sept. 21, 2007)
Petrotiger Limited		United States v. Hammarskjold, No. 13-cr-2086 (D.N.J. Nov. 8, 2013); United States v. Sigelman, No. 13-cr-2087 (D.N.J. Nov. 8, 2013); United States v. Weisman, No. 13-cr-730 (D.N.J. Nov. 8, 2013)

Case Name	SEC Case Citation	DOJ Case Citation
Pride International Incorporated	SEC v. Pride Int'l Inc., No. 10-cv-4335 (S.D. Tex. Nov. 4, 2010)	United States v. Pride Int'l Inc., No. 410-cr-766 (S.D. Tex. Nov. 4, 2010)
Ralph Lauren Corporation	SEC v. Ralph Lauren Corp., Non-Prosecution Agreement (Apr. 22, 2013)	Non-Pros. Agreement, In re Ralph Lauren Corp. (Apr. 22, 2013)
Royal Dutch Shell Public Limited Company	In the Matter of Royal Dutch Shell plc, Exchange Act Release No. 63243 (Nov. 4, 2010)	United States v. Shell Nigeria Exploration and Production Co. Ltd., No. 10-cr-767 (S.D. Tex. Nov. 4, 2010)
Siemens Aktiengesellschaft	SEC v. Siemens Aktiengesellschaft, No. 08-cv-2167 (D.D.C. Dec. 12, 2008)	United States v. Siemens Aktiengesellschaft, No. 08-cr-367 (D.D.C. Dec. 12, 2008)
Stryker Corporation	In the Matter of Stryker Corp., Exchange Act Release No. 70751 (Oct. 24, 2013)	
Terra Telecommunications Corporation		United States v. Cruz, et al., No. 09-cr-21010 (S.D. Fla. July 13, 2011)
Tidewater Incorporated	SEC v. Tidewater, Inc., No. 10-cv-4180 (E.D. La. Nov. 4, 2010)	United States v. Tidewater Marine Int'l, Inc., No. 10-cr-770 (S.D. Tex. Nov. 4, 2010)
Total Société Anonyme	In the Matter of Total, S.A., Exchange Act Release No. 69654 (May 29, 2013)	United States v. Total, S.A., 13-cr-239 (E.D. Va. May 29, 2013)
Transocean Incorporated	SEC v. Transocean Inc., No. 10-cv-1891 (D.D.C. Nov. 4, 2010)	United States v. Transocean, Inc., No. 10-cr-768 (S.D. Tex. Nov. 4, 2010)
Tyson Foods Incorporated	SEC v. Tyson Foods, Inc., No. 11-cv-350 (D.D.C. Feb. 10, 2011)	United States v. Tyson Foods, Inc., No. 11-cr-37 (D.D.C. Feb. 10, 2011)
Willbros Group Incorporated	SEC v. Willbros Group, Inc., et al., No. 08-cv-1494 (S.D. Tex. May 14, 2008)	United States v. Willbros Group, Inc., et al., No. 08-cr-287 (S.D. Tex. May 14, 2008)

Chapter 1

Introduction: Latin American Compliance Bridges

In 2011, U.S. company Tyson Foods reached a US$5.2 million set-
tlement with the U.S. Department of Justice ("DOJ") and the U.S.
Securities and Exchange Commission ("the SEC") admitting to
violations of the U.S. Foreign Corrupt Practices Act ("FCPA") by
its Mexican subsidiary, Tyson de Mexico. The subsidiary had paid
US$350,000 in bribes over 12 years to Mexican veterinary officials
responsible for inspecting and certifying meat products for export. It
did this by accepting phony invoices from the inspectors and putting
the veterinarians' wives on the payroll, even though the wives performed no work. As part of the settlement, the company committed
to enhancing its anti-corruption compliance program overseas in
Mexico and Brazil, where it had production facilities. When issuing its press release, the company emphasized that none of the meat

products exported from Tyson de Mexico had been shipped to the United States, and that no exported products had any safety issues.

The Tyson case highlights many issues common to FCPA enforcement, including parent companies being held legally responsible for the corrupt acts of their foreign subsidiaries; sources of public corruption that go well beyond typical government contracting and public procurement activity; and creative bribery schemes involving multiple actors. Perhaps most notable, however, was the lack of sensitivity that Tyson demonstrated to Mexican audiences in its response to the findings. Mexicans were left asking, "If the meat subject to questionable health inspection did not go to the United States, then where did it go? Was it sold internally in the Mexican market?" Those of us who work in anti-corruption compliance were also left wondering, if Tyson was serious about building a culture of compliance within its Latin American workforces, wouldn't it have been sensible to acknowledge Latin Americans' health concerns, too?

Such a disconnect between a company's approach to anti-corruption compliance and the realities of compliance implementation on the ground in foreign countries is common today. Notions of corporate compliance are still new and emerging, and companies headquartered in the United States often struggle to develop successful strategies to implement their codes of conduct and policies in distant countries. In Latin America, in particular, U.S. companies tend to confront cultural, historical, geographical, and language barriers when implementing programs that involve their neighbors to the South. These obstacles affect not only the quality of the compliance program. They also can create roadblocks when companies must conduct internal investigations of alleged cross-border corporate malfeasance involving the region.

Similarly, companies based in Latin America are expanding internationally and also face challenges with corporate compliance. More and more, these companies are seeking to learn about, and adopt, the compliance standards that are now more commonplace at U.S. companies. Sometimes, to them, these standards can appear foreign, new, and odd. As a result, companies in the region have begun inventing their own ways to make programs work. In some cases, they are doing so proactively. In others, the market is demanding these changes. For less fortunate companies, their interest in compliance comes as a result of enforcement of the FCPA by U.S. authorities, demonstrating the unexpectedly broad reach of the law across jurisdictions to companies and individuals in Latin America.

Over the last 10 years working on anti-corruption compliance and enforcement issues in Latin America, I have learned effective strategies to help bridge the cultural and business divides that can be typical in the anti-corruption profession. For those facing similar challenges, this book aims to shrink the gap between the two worlds. It sets out to clarify common FCPA misconceptions, describe prevalent Latin American corruption risks, offer examples of effective compliance strategies in the region, and provide Latin American examples of emerging compliance best practices. It follows a basic premise: Since the legal prohibitions of the FCPA are international by their very nature, responding to FCPA risk should be international, too.

— —

International anti-corruption law is the most cutting-edge area of international law today, putting those who practice it at the intersection of traditional legal disciplines, business considerations, cultural aspects, governance issues, and human rights. Successful practitioners must realize and appreciate the interrelated nature of the work—a valuable lesson I have learned over my years in Latin America.

Take as an example one case I investigated in a Mexican jungle where multimillion dollar kickbacks were being funneled to officials of Petróleos Mexicanos ("Pemex") through a mom-and-pop services company in a town where the average monthly salary was less than US$1,500. While interviewing witnesses and reviewing e-mails of those believed to be involved in the activities, I could not help but think about the dramatic inequalities that these schemes reinforced. I thought about the challenges posed to businesses operating there that wanted to stay clean and the wasted resources that otherwise could have gone to the public good. It seemed so unnecessary, for example, that the roads in the town remained half-finished and pot-hole-ridden, or that our plane could not land on the runway after a heavy rain. Understanding this context with a level of sensitivity, in turn, helped me manage the fact-gathering process more effectively. People seemed more willing to share stories about the underlying conduct and describe relevant documentation.

On another case in which I found myself interviewing miners alleged to have given improper payments to local community leaders in a lawless section of northern Colombia, the cultural barriers could not have been more obvious for me—a blond haired, blue-eyed guy from Texas. What I learned, however, was that by engaging the interviewees in Spanish, appreciating the art of listening over talking, and being honest and upfront about the nature of our review and my purpose for being there, I was able to break down walls that otherwise would have made it impossible for the company to get to the truth about what happened.

Another piece of advice I have picked up over the years: one should never underestimate the sophistication of bribery schemes that occur in Latin America. This lesson I learned while untangling a highly complex bribery scheme in the urban maze of São Paulo that involved several high-profile global companies, including Brazilian-based companies, engaged in cutthroat international competition, and government officials from no less than three different state and federal agencies.

These experiences in Latin America have taught me valuable lessons about responding to the growing web of transnational anti-corruption laws. The center of this web is the FCPA. The U.S. federal statute addressing bribery of government officials located outside of the United States is still the most important law pushing companies and their leaders to be more ethical and inspiring innovations in corporate governance and compliance. In the short history of active FCPA enforcement, the escalation of which occurred in the early-to-mid 2000s, U.S. authorities have applied the law to no fewer than 70 different bribery schemes involving Latin America. Enforcement of the FCPA has spanned 15 countries throughout the region. The only major Latin American countries that have not been affected by FCPA enforcement, that are publicly known about (U.S. authorities' decisions to drop cases are not always publicized) are El Salvador, Paraguay, and Uruguay. Latin American businesspeople, and more than one Latin American public official, have been charged in the United States with FCPA-related violations.

U.S. authorities are currently pursuing some of the region's largest companies, including Petrobras, Eletrobras, and Embraer, for possible FCPA violations. The Petrobras case is notable for many reasons, first and foremost because of its enormity. It is alleged that, from 2004 to 2014, some of the largest Brazilian and international companies, said to be organized in cartels, paid bribes to high-profile Petrobras officials and other public officials in exchange for billions of dollars in contracts with Petrobras, Brazil's largest company. The companies are alleged to have shaved billions of dollars off the value of contracts in the form of kickbacks to the executives and politicians. The U.S. authorities launched investigations of the company. By the end of 2015, Brazilian authorities had charged 173 individuals and convicted 75, recovered US$1.7 billion in bribe payments, and responded to 85 requests for international cooperation from 37 different countries. The investigation had implicated 30 other companies in sectors as diverse as engineering and banking, and Petrobras had written down nearly US$17 billion due to the findings to date. By the end of 2015, there were even indications that the matter had the potential of bringing down the president and the economy of Latin America's largest country.

The FCPA has affected the Latin American region in other ways, too. The OECD Convention on Combating Bribery of Foreign Public Officials in International Business Transactions ("OECD Anti-Bribery Convention"), the provisions of which are largely modeled after the FCPA, has driven more than 40 of the world's most developed economies to adopt anti-bribery laws. Five of those countries—soon to be six—are in Latin America: Argentina, Brazil, Chile, Colombia, and Mexico. Peru is next.

Enforcement of the FCPA also has motivated global companies to develop strict anti-corruption compliance programs. On a day-to-day basis, these programs are impacting how personnel are doing business on the ground, the types of interactions they have with Latin American government officials, the local business partners they choose to embrace, and the service providers they choose to engage.

These are all not trivial developments, especially for a region where corruption is often perceived as institutionalized. Whether one looks at global indexes, follows local press reports, or hears personal stories of experiences on the ground, corruption often seems integrated into the political and commercial order of many parts of Latin America. In the 2016 Latin America Corruption Survey conducted by Miller & Chevalier in partnership with 13 law firms throughout the region, about half of the 625 respondents described corruption as a "significant obstacle" to doing business in the region. More than half said they believed their companies had lost business in the region to competitors paying bribes. Only about 10% of those who believed their companies lost business said they reported the issues to local authorities. And less than a third of those respondents said that the government investigated the matter. These findings show perceptions of notably high levels of corruption and lack of faith in local governments to address the problems. Even more striking, these findings are consistent with the responses received when Miller & Chevalier asked the same questions in surveys in 2008 and again in 2012, suggesting enduring risks and ossified attitudes.

Similarly, in its 2014 Worldwide Governance Indicators assessment, the World Bank ranked Latin American countries, on average, in the 52nd percentile worldwide for "Control of Corruption." The ranking defined the concept as "perceptions of the extent to which public power is exercised for private gain, including both petty and grand forms of corruption, as well as 'capture' of the state by elites and private interests." To measure the concept, the World Bank considered a host of variables, including the level of public trust in politicians, and the prevalence of irregular payments in exports, imports, public utilities, tax collection, public contracts, and judicial decisions. In Transparency International's 2015 Corrupt Perceptions Index ("CPI"), 85% of Latin American countries scored below 50 out of 100, where zero is highly corrupt and 100 is very clean.

Indeed, the forms that corruption takes in the region may vary depending on the sector at issue, the geography where business is conducted, the history of relations between government and society, and the government systems in place. What doesn't change, however, is the general threat that corrupt activity poses to ethical business. The pernicious effect of corruption on Latin American societies is unmistakable, frustrating the rule of law, misguiding public resources, inhibiting free markets from achieving greater efficiencies, and undermining the ability of states to address critical issues like poverty alleviation, improved education, environmental protection, and national security.

Despite all the challenges that corruption presents in Latin America today, reasons abound to be upbeat about the future. Today, in various markets in the region, one can feel the quiet rumblings of reform as local companies embrace modern governance structures. Anti-corruption compliance conferences that were thinly attended only three years ago are now overflowing in places like Brazil, Mexico, and Colombia. Business communities in countries like Argentina and Peru are waking up to the legal threats of corrupt acts and learning about international compliance standards. Independent compliance organizations are being established in countries throughout the region, even in markets as small as that of Ecuador. The 2016 Latin America Corruption Survey found that increasing numbers of people working in the region are familiar with the FCPA. In 2012, 65% of respondents were familiar with the law, while in 2016 the percentage had gone up to almost three-quarters. Even more interesting is the fact that almost 75% of non-U.S. respondents to the survey in 2016 were "very familiar" or "somewhat familiar" with the FCPA, demonstrating the growing impact the law is having in the region.

Some data appears to reinforce the notion that corruption is slightly ebbing in many Latin American countries. According to Transparency International's CPI, over the past decade perceived corruption has decreased in Argentina, Bolivia, Brazil, Costa Rica, Cuba, the Dominican Republic, Ecuador, Guatemala, Honduras, Nicaragua, Panama, Paraguay, and Peru.

To be sure, the CPI is only a proxy for understanding actual corruption risk in different countries; corruption is usually conducted in secret and therefore difficult to measure. Nevertheless, the CPI enjoys significant international legitimacy by drawing on corruption assessments and surveys from a dozen reputable institutions so that each country's score is reinforced by multiple sources. Better CPI scores have been shown to have a significant positive correlation with economic growth, as well as a significant negative correlation with other proxies for corruption, such as overabundance of regulation and black-market activity. Significant changes in a country's score can meaningfully reflect changes in perceive corruption, especially if change is sustained over several years rather than a mere one- or two-year fluctuation.

When considering regional trends, one sees that U.S. enforcement officials aren't the only cops on the global anti-corruption beat either. Local jurisdictions are strengthening their own laws and starting to enforce them, too. The bribery investigation of Brazilian airline manufacturer Embraer, for example, began with an FCPA subpoena from U.S. authorities in 2010, but Brazilian authorities quickly got involved. A few years later, it was Brazilian authorities who first launched the investigation of Petrobras before the United States initiated an FCPA investigation. This was a striking development that turned on its head the usual pattern in which U.S. authorities initiate an inquiry and other governments then follow suit.

Some aspects of this revolution are not so quiet. The dramatic buildup to the adoption of the Brazilian Clean Companies Act ("BCCA") in 2013 is a good example. Two years previously, Brazilian President Dilma Rousseff had ousted numerous cabinet members for alleged corruption, a set of presidential actions that might have been unheard of in earlier times. One year before that, the Brazilian Supreme Court upheld the guilty convictions of dozens of public officials and business leaders in the *mensalão* ("big monthly payment") scandal, the largest corruption trial in the country's history. These public officials and business leaders had been involved in a scheme to pay Brazilian congressional deputies approximately US$12,000 in "monthly payments" in exchange for favorable voting.

At the same time, other changes were afoot. Brazil's Congress was amending its anti-money laundering law, increasing fines and broadening predicate offenses, and the scope of persons obligated to report suspicious activities. The country's Access to Information law also took effect, creating heightened transparency standards for the use of public funds. Against this backdrop, the Brazilian Congress had proposed new anti-corruption legislation that would, for the first time, make companies liable for the corrupt acts of their executives and employees. The purpose of the legislation was to bring Brazil's legal framework in line with its commitments as a signatory to the OECD Anti-Bribery Convention. The legislation stalled for three years until the Brazilian House of Representatives finally approved it on April 24, 2013. The legislation, under fierce opposition, then remained in limbo in the Brazilian senate—that is until June 2013, when more than one million Brazilian citizens took to the streets in mass protest, sparked by a heightened frustration with government corruption. In the wake of this upheaval, the Brazilian senate approved the BCCA on July 4th before President Rousseff signed it into law on August 1, 2013.

Though the most dramatic changes have occurred in Brazil, it is not the only hot spot for reform in the region. Similar protests are occurring now in Mexico, harnessing the power of social media to rally public support as citizens grow frustrated by the apparent complicit nature of local authorities with cartels and revelations that the Mexican president's wife received financing for an extravagant house from someone who happened to win a billion dollar train construction project. As a result, the Mexican congress and state legislatures approved a constitutional amendment in 2015 that will allow for the adoption of a new National Anti-Corruption System, planned to occur in 2016. In Venezuela, public dissatisfaction with government inefficiency and corruption is at a boiling point, with parliamentary elections in 2015 going to the opposition party in a resounding victory. The president of Guatemala resigned and was arrested in 2015 after public outcry over his involvement and the involvement of several other high-level officials in a systematic scheme to siphon funds from tax payments at customs. Different parts of Latin America, to different degrees, similarly are toying with the idea of establishing or bolstering their own anti-corruption enforcement regimes.

Common Misconceptions

Latin Americans are often surprised to learn about multilateral anti-bribery enforcement and are equally surprised to learn about the broad extraterritorial reach of the FCPA. The steady stream of blockbuster foreign bribery fines—such as Alstom (US$772 million), Avon (US$135 million), Alcoa (US$384 million), and Total (US$398 million)—particularly attract interest and attention. People in the region want to hear about how individuals can be personally liable, and the aggressive ways in which U.S. enforcers are pursuing their cases through the use of wiretaps, body wires, border searches, and physical surveillance.

Given these dynamics, perhaps an appropriate starting point for this book is to describe the most frequent reactions I hear when discussing Latin American FCPA work with peers. In general, these reactions reflect misconceptions about this new area of international law. The discussions differ, however, depending on whether they occur in the United States or in Latin America. But they all shed light on some of the prevailing attitudes toward this new legal paradigm. Crafting answers to these questions is a good starting point to building anti-corruption compliance bridges between the two regions.

Misconception #1: "Isn't corruption just part of Latin American culture?"

No culture embraces corruption. No population inherently accepts a structure to society where their leaders steal from them in a permissible way. No matter one's background, violating the public trust to benefit personally is distasteful, lacking in honor, and unethical – and all people inherently understand this, including those in Latin America.

Alexandra Wrage, President of Trace International, a business compliance group, often has said that corruption occurs when opportunity is combined with insufficient penalties. In such environments, where enforcement is lacking, officials are more likely to seek bribes, and the general public has less ability for recourse, she says. If this is the case, then it is wrong to confuse tolerance of something that is out of one's control with endorsement of the practice. Controlling corruption is, therefore, not culture-dependent but rather a function of increasing the negative consequences that result from corrupt acts. The risks associated with engaging in bribery need to be visible and credible to those who contemplate giving or receiving improper payments.

Evidencing this truth are the frequent national protests in Brazil, Mexico, Guatemala, and Venezuela. They show quite the opposite of a preference for corruption. They demonstrate, in a resounding way, popular discontent with political corruption. They remind us that corruption persists when there are inadequate means to fight it. They show that suppressed frustrations can be explosive when people are finally given a voice.

Not surprisingly, the notion that some cultures are inherently more corrupt than others is also offensive to people from the "more corrupt" cultures. If you were to ask someone on the streets of Buenos Aires, Argentina, or Guayaquil, Ecuador if they approve of their officials accepting bribes, few, if any, would reply "yes." People in countries with high corruption bear the personal impact of procurement officials who select low quality goods, such as expired medicines or shoddily constructed bridges, in exchange for kickbacks. They are affected when government inspectors ignore food safety concerns while getting a cut of the profits from the food producer. They are aggravated when city clerks issue driver's licenses only to those willing to give tips, or teachers give transcripts only to those willing to provide favors. They might not always understand what goes on behind the curtain of bribery schemes, but they intuitively feel the effects. Shoddy government has real results in day-to-day life.

In an age of transnational bribery laws, using the excuse of a corrupt "culture" not only demonstrates ignorance but also can be dangerous. For example, a 2012 Pulitzer Prize winning *New York Times* article about alleged bribery by Wal-Mart employees in Mexico suggests that U.S. Wal-Mart executives held these types of views. These employees were reported to say that bribery was a Mexican issue and better left to Mexican responses. The article describes a prevailing sense among Wal-Mart executives that international business involves moral ambiguities and that to think otherwise is naïve. This viewpoint, if true, disregards Mexican law, which prohibits bribery. It ignores the vast majority of Mexicans who consider bribery unethical and unacceptable. It is also inconsistent with the viewpoints of FCPA enforcement officials, who have been investigating Wal-Mart's overseas practices since 2011.

Even if certain cultures tend to have greater tolerance for bribery because of the lack of recourse, these cultural considerations are irrelevant when it comes to FCPA enforcement. No matter how commonplace bribery is in a country, this fact does not create a civil or criminal defense under the FCPA.

Some argue that bribery is built into local economies. The tax collector, for example, may be forced to demand bribes when not paid enough on which to live, just as a local police officer may feel compelled to do so to feed her family. One can certainly have sympathy for this perspective. The receipt of bribes does have a human side, especially as it relates to petty corruption. I have seen it firsthand when asked for bribes in places like Brazil, Argentina, and Tajikistan. Some requests are less about greed and more about trying to ensure a basic livelihood.

Even taking into consideration the human side, corruption is still criminal in almost every, if not all, countries. The plight of low-level officials highlights not the need for more bribes, but the need for improved state systems. A company that wants to change such systems to improve the business environment has other options aside from bribery, including working with foreign governments directly to help fund and oversee programs that better train and equip local police forces to perform their duties. The DOJ, itself, in an opinion release, explicitly permitted a company to provide financial support to the customs department of an African country as part of a pilot project to improve the effectiveness of local law enforcement. The company had trained the officials to better identify and prevent the import and export of counterfeit goods. In turn, this helped the company address its own immediate market threat. This type of action differs greatly from an approach that turns a blind eye on foreign bribery, which serves only to fuel a system based on kickbacks.

Misconception #2: "Isn't the FCPA bad for business?"

Another reaction I hear in the United States is that the FCPA undermines U.S. business interests abroad. Although the FCPA prohibits U.S. companies from pursuing certain strategies to generate business in foreign markets, that view is shortsighted and misses the larger picture. Business growth based on the payment of bribes tends to create more problems than it solves. For one, officials will always ask for more. There is a "feed the bears" mentality that does little more than get companies into trouble. If companies must "out-bribe" their competition, they will face greater challenge and uncertainty. Tolerance of corruption gives bureaucrats an incentive to create more choke points at which they can extract even more benefits. A one-step process suddenly becomes a four-step process – with the request for four payments. Moreover, contracts based on improper payments are often unsustainable. Siemens learned this the hard way. It paid millions of dollars in improper payments for a billion dollar public contract that never came to fruition in Argentina. A business strategy based on bribery also risks increasingly more legal liability for the companies and their personnel, as more jurisdictions continue to enhance their anti-corruption laws.

Companies need stable and predictable markets for business to grow. When corruption flourishes, it undermines government institutions and faith in the political and economic order. When left unaddressed, these frustrations can erupt, as they have in Brazil, Venezuela, and Guatemala, as well as parts of the Arab world, creating instability and disruption. By countering corruption instead, countries make markets more fair, more stable, and ultimately more profitable.

Of course, U.S. companies should not be put at a disadvantage in global markets and should not be expected to follow stricter rules than those of other countries. To be fair, however, the FCPA applies to foreign entities as well as U.S. companies – and attempts to reach them. If a non-U.S. company has shares publicly listed in the United States, or if it or its officials take action in the United States in furtherance of a bribery scheme, or conspire to violate the law with a company that is subject to the FCPA, the non-U.S. company or individual can be subject to enforcement and prosecution, even if they never enter the United States. In fact, FCPA actions against non-U.S. companies are now commonplace. As of 2015, eight of the 10 most expensive FCPA enforcement actions were brought against non-U.S. companies. Non-U.S. companies including Alcatel, Bridgestone, Embraer, Panalpina, and Petrobras have all been subject to FCPA investigations for their activities in Latin America.

Misconception #3: "The FCPA wrongly targets foreigners; you have corruption in the United States, too."

In Latin America, I almost always hear this reaction when speaking about the FCPA. People are surprised and defensive that the FCPA applies only to bribery of non-U.S. officials. They see it as a lopsided approach to addressing corruption.

True, there is certainly corruption in the United States. U.S. politicians have been caught committing such acts, both in the past and in recent history. Louisiana Congressman William Jefferson was charged with hiding a stack of cash from kickbacks in his freezer. California Congressman Duke Cunningham lived rent-free on a yacht gifted by a defense-contracting firm. Illinois Governor Rod Blagojevich attempted to sell the U.S. Senate seat vacated by President Barack Obama. What is important to highlight, however, is that the United States has strong domestic bribery laws to address these types of local bribery issues. That U.S. Congress created the FCPA to apply only to bribes paid to officials from other parts of the world does not suggest that preventing domestic bribery is not addressed forcefully under U.S. law.

When attempting to compare anti-corruption efforts in the United States with those in Latin America, it is relevant to acknowledge that corruption exists everywhere, no matter the country. But some countries have done a better job of addressing it. Those with stronger government institutions find more effective ways of criminalizing public corruption and penalizing the culprits. This results in lower levels of impunity for those who choose to give and receive bribes. When the calculation of the likelihood and consequences of being caught changes, behavior tends to change.

At the same time, no matter how stringent a country's anti-corruption laws, bribery cannot be prevented one hundred percent of the time. The more relevant question is how a company, or a country, responds to the practice. Is bribery something that is institutionalized, or is it treated as an exception to the norm? When bribes are offered or requested, do the people involved feel threatened by the possibility of being caught, or do they commit such acts with a sense of impunity, or even justification? Perhaps the answers to these questions are the biggest differentiator between a country like the United States, where corruption is seen more as the exception, and many parts of Latin America, where a bribe might not be out of the norm.

People in Latin America will understandably ask why lobbying in the United States is not considered a form of bribery. Indeed, it is hard to argue with the proposition that egregious lobbying has become commonplace in our country. By some, the practice certainly could be seen as an institutionalized form of corruption. The difference between lobbying and illicit bribery, however, is that many forms of lobbying common in our political process have been approved through a democratic lawmaking process. Elected representatives have decided that certain types of paid political influence are acceptable, legitimate, and legal. Furthermore, these kinds of payments are generally regulated. In this respect, lobbying differs from rampant and unlawful corruption that is unlawful.

Misconception #4: "The FCPA is misguided; you can't end corruption in Latin America."

When speaking with Latin Americans about the efforts of the U.S. Government and other governments to curb corruption, people in the region tend to express so much skepticism. Some of it is understandable. To consider a world free of corruption is a far-fetched proposition. Certainly, everyone would be better off if transparency were the norm and officials conducted themselves as expected. However, greed is a natural human instinct, and the world has never, and will never, find a way to completely eradicate the desire of public officials to seek private gain.

The purpose of the international anti-corruption movement might be thought of more as an effort to move corruption from a place where it is institutionalized and incorporated into the fabric of society, to a place where bribery, when it occurs, is the exception and carries serious consequences. The goal is to decrease the sense of impunity among the public sector.

Because of strong and sustained enforcement of the FCPA, and due to a collection of other important factors that are discussed in this book, the institutionalized nature of corruption in Latin America has started to fragment.

—— ——

These are exciting times to be a participant in a quickly developing area of law. To be sure, the international anti-corruption movement is not just a fad. Companies are being penalized with ever-increasing fines. Public officials are going to jail, and corporate leaders are enhancing their companies' anti-corruption compliance programs to meet evolving standards. Expect these developments to continue.

As this book demonstrates, the shift toward criminalizing bribery in Latin America is real. To watch it play out is something remarkable. To participate in it, whether through representing U.S. companies which are doing business in the region or working with Latin American companies going global, is thrilling. Businesspeople, public officials, and compliance professionals are quickly embracing global standards. This book sets out to provide a snapshot of this monumental development.

Most importantly, these chapters help guide compliance practitioners in forming critical links between two different regions. Kathryn C. Atkinson, chair of Miller & Chevalier's International Department, describes the challenge as one of "pushing past preconceptions and implicit or explicit biases to see that people from all backgrounds can support anti-corruption standards, and can continually do better at corporate governance." Others describe it as taming the wild world of cross-border business. I describe it as building bridges between distant cultures that globalization has now intimately linked together.

Chapter 2

Latin America: A Melting Pot of Corruption Risks

Massive in land size and population, Latin America boasts more than half a billion people and 24 different nations, each with its own diverse culture. In addition to Spanish, Portuguese, French, and English, Latin Americans speak hundreds of other indigenous languages. And the cultures found in Paraguay, for example, are not the same as those found in Panama. Even within individual countries, the geographic diversity can be staggering. Brazil alone boasts the natural jungle of Manaus and the concrete jungle of São Paulo. Mexico, too, features industrialized Monterrey and indigenous Chiapas.

With so much diversity, it is impossible to generalize about corruption risks in the region. As some are known to say, "Latin America is not a country." Consider that Argentina and Chile share the longest border in South America, but the two countries could not be further apart in terms of corruption risk. In 2015, Chile earned a CPI score of 70 out of a possible 100 (23rd out of 167 countries ranked), which puts it at about 86th percentile worldwide. In contrast, Argentina ranked 107th with a CPI score of 32, which puts it at about 36th percentile.

The forms of corruption risk encountered in Latin America are equally diverse, as evidenced by the many FCPA enforcement actions involving Latin American countries. Some schemes have included bread-and-butter, straightforward payments to offshore shell companies to win public contracts in underdeveloped countries. For example, executives in the Terra Telecommunications case used shell companies to pay US$890,000 to officials from the Haitian state-owned telecommunications monopoly. Other schemes, in comparison, have included highly sophisticated structures involving multiple actors colluding throughout the world to rig billion dollar public contracts in more developed countries. For example, executives in the Siemens Argentina case used an elaborate network of Argentine, Bahamian, Emirati, German, and Uruguayan individuals and consulting firms to channel more than US$105 million to Argentine officials to win contracts to produce the country's national identification card.

Additionally, risks can vary depending on whether a company operates in a rural or urban environment. Within Colombia, for example, rural operations might involve "security payment" requests while business in Bogotá might involve complicated public procurements risks. The type of government in the country can also dictate the type of risks companies might encounter. In Venezuela, the government takes an active role in the economy, which means that companies more regularly interact with individuals considered "officials" under anti-corruption laws, creating a higher likelihood of bribery risk. Chile, on the other hand, is known for its market-friendly approach to the private sector, where business interactions with the government are less frequent, reducing the opportunity for public corruption.

Corruption risks can also depend on the level of concentration of wealth and power in a country. As noted in a 2015 article in *The Economist*, family companies in Latin America have historically cultivated political connections as an antidote to weak property rights and government interference. As a result, wealth and power are highly concentrated, there is a greater risk of regulatory capture, and a small elite regularly moves in and out of government and the private sector. This makes it more likely that, when a foreign company partners with a local company or uses a local third party, a member of that entity could be a former congressperson or married to a military general. Countries where power is decentralized and multi-faceted—such as Mexico, Colombia, Brazil, and Argentina—usually create a different set of issues. Companies might be required to seek a series of approvals from several different government entities to sign off on a license renewal. They might need to consult local experts who know how to navigate dense procurement processes, which can create a different kind of third-party risk.

Such variety in corruption risk heightens the need for companies to conduct formal risk assessments on which to base their compliance strategies, and periodically update those assessments.

To respond to corruption threats, companies must understand them first. In fact, U.S. enforcement officials consider formal risk assessments to be a fundamental component of a company's anti-corruption compliance program. They instruct companies to consider a list of factors when assessing risk, including the specific country, industry or sector, and nature of government interactions in executing business. Companies should consider the risks that third-party intermediaries create by virtue of the work they do on the company's behalf. They should also consider the risks created by joint venture partners.

While it is impossible to make sweeping generalizations of corruption risks in Latin America, it is helpful to be alert to certain risk themes that tend to arise over and over again in the region. These themes are listed below, as well as suggestions for compliance strategies companies should consider to address them.

Public Procurement Manipulation

Public procurement is the most common source of corruption risk no matter where a company does business in the world. That finding is supported by a Foreign Bribery Report published in December 2014 by the OECD, which measured transnational corruption based on data from the 427 total foreign bribery cases that had been investigated, prosecuted, and concluded since the OECD Anti-Bribery Convention entered into force in 1999. According to that report, 57% of cases involved bribes related to public procurements.

Latin America is no exception, as demonstrated by several FCPA cases involving public procurement. For example, in 2010, French telecommunications conglomerate Alcatel-Lucent paid US$92 million in penalties in connection with bribes to Costa Rican officials in the early 2000s to win mobile telephone contracts. Similarly, in 2012, Eli Lilly paid US$29 million in penalties for bribes paid by the company's Brazilian distributor to win local government contracts for pharmaceuticals. In 2012, aircraft maintenance provider BizJet paid US$11.8 million in penalties in connection with bribes paid to Mexican, Panamanian, and Brazilian officials to obtain aircraft maintenance services, including for the Mexican presidential fleet.

Government procurement often occurs through state-owned enterprises, such as national oil companies and public hospitals. Out of all areas of government, respondents to the 2016 Latin America Corruption Survey rated state-owned companies throughout the region as presenting one of the highest levels of corruption, with 93% of respondents describing "significant" or "moderate" corruption associated with the state-owned companies with which they engage.

Large amounts of money are at stake when governments procure roads, computer systems, oil extraction services, medical equipment, power stations, and textbooks, because companies and their representatives must interact directly with government officials, who have pockets of discretion that can create space for manipulation of official procurement processes. When corruption is involved, procurement decisions are no longer based on price, experience, and quality, but are based on how the government official can benefit.

Below are some common ways in which schemes have been organized in Latin America:

➤ Procurement officials require bidders to hire "consultants" as a way to funnel money back to the officials.

➤ Companies disguise direct payments to procurement officials as something else. For example, a company may award contracts to doctors of state-owned hospitals in charge of procuring goods, purportedly for them to conduct trainings that never actually occur.

➤ Companies hire "experts" who, with or without the company's knowledge, previously worked for the procurement agency itself, still have contacts in the procurement office, and might have even designed the actual specifications of the tender at issue. As former officials, they know how to game the system.

➤ Improper payments, if promised or made during the project design phase, influence procurement authorities to narrowly design a project's specifications to benefit the company making the payments.

➤ Project designers proactively seek to include complicated technical features in the tender. The more technical, the more room an official has to use discretion in the selection process to favor one bidder over another.

➤ Companies gain access to confidential information, such as being able to see the tender specifications before they are officially released or gaining access to a competitor's confidential bid information and then revising ..ir own bids accordingly to win.

➤ Procurement officials choose to fully vet the bid of one company while giving a less rigorous review to the bid of another. In this way, kickback-paying companies that are unable to show appropriate qualifications and experience or the ability to deliver the appropriate product are still able to win the contract.

➤ Companies learn early on that a government agency is considering the procurement of goods and will then seek to "entertain" procurement officials before the tender process begins. During these periods, actors are able to develop complicated schemes to transfer improper payments and direct contracts in return.

The World Bank, which finances projects and has jurisdiction to investigate and sanction companies and businesspeople in the projects that engage in wrongdoing, has published a list of "The Most Common Red Flags of Fraud and Corruption in Procurement" for its investigators and staff. The guide serves as a useful resource for chief compliance officers, as well. For example, suspicions should arise when a procurement authority does not select the lowest bidder, repeatedly awards contracts to the same bidder, or changes the contract terms and values after the process concludes. Processes should be suspect when one company repeatedly wins government contracts with values just under procurement thresholds, a losing bidder becomes a subcontractor, or the prices of goods seem inflated.

When these "red flags" occur, compliance teams should take a closer look. Companies should make sure they know and follow the rules of public procurements that specific countries have in place. They should know when it is appropriate to revise or clarify their bids. They should know and comply with timelines for submitting bids, submitting clarification questions, and expecting procurement decisions.

Regulatory Risks

Compared to other regions of the world, Latin American countries are recognized as having regulatory regimes of poor quality. The World Bank's 2015 Doing Business Report ranks Latin American countries, on average, in the bottom half worldwide for regulatory quality. The report compares 189 economies by measuring the clarity, predictability, and efficiency of regulations that apply to areas like construction permits, regulating electricity, registering property, obtaining credit, protecting investors, and paying taxes. In practice, Latin American regulatory regimes are often found to be vague, overlapping, or enforced by multiple government agencies. This picture seems unlikely to change for the foreseeable future. While Colombia, Paraguay, and Peru have seen their scores for regulatory quality improve in recent years, overall Latin American countries' scores have fallen, particularly in countries like Bolivia, Cuba, and Venezuela.

Regulatory quality and corruption risk may be directly linked. The more ambiguity in the law, the more opportunity there is for corruption to occur. Ambiguity and complexity create the potential for authorities to use discretion in decision-making, creating greater opportunity for manipulation of government processes, which can form the basis of corrupt acts. In addition, the more government actors who are involved in a regulatory process, the more places where bribe requests or payments can occur.

Opaque regulations can not only create opportunities for officials to demand bribes, but also incentives for company officials to offer them. When a permit is caught in a regulatory black hole and the government is not responding, an employee might feel pressure to offer a benefit to "encourage" officials to act. Depending on the circumstances, this might or might not constitute a permissible facilitating payment under the FCPA.

Regulatory hurdles are common for companies operating in the region. To build its stores in Mexico, Wal-Mart had to obtain various types of zoning licenses, environmental permits, neighborhood association approvals, and other regulatory requirements. The ongoing FCPA investigation of the company is said to focus on alleged payments the company made to speed up these processes, or to circumvent them. The Tyson Foods case, discussed in the Introduction to this book, is an example of health and safety inspection requirements that the company made payments to circumvent.

Due to the complexity of regulatory regimes, hiring local third parties who know how to navigate local rules may be necessary. Companies commonly use *despachantes* ("dispatchers") in Brazil to work through complex webs of rules. The World Bank's 2014 Doing Business Report ranks Brazil 169th out of 189 economies in "ease of dealing with construction permits," with 18 procedures requiring

426 days on average. In Mexico, companies use *gestores* ("managers"), a well-established profession of service providers who manage hurdles in difficult regulatory environments. Without proper vetting and controls, use of these types of third parties creates risk that they will make improper payments on a company's behalf.

Muddy regulations might also have the potential to trip up a company's internal investigation into allegations of FCPA violations, discussed in detail in Chapter 8. When laws seem unclear, a company's interactions with the government might create the appearance of impropriety, even when no improper payments in fact occurred. Or it might be difficult to determine if a company's personnel actually broke local law.

Companies can manage these risks in various ways. For example, by consulting local counsel to gain a clearer understanding of the exact nature of the applicable law, companies can ensure they stay on the right side of the law when paying regulatory fees. In internal investigations, a company might want to give heightened attention to its regulatory interactions. Compliance training can target employees who handle regulatory interactions to ensure they are aware of the added risks associated with their work and know to spot and report red flags when they see them.

Risks at Customs

Customs-related bribery risks are common in Latin America. Understaffed ports lead to paperwork and decision bottlenecks, creating incentives for some companies to provide favors to officials to skip lines. Underpaid customs officials might have an incentive to seek illicit rents simply to earn a living wage. Companies with perishable goods, in particular, might feel pressure to give into officials' demands to not lose their product while awaiting customs clearance. Customs brokers with expertise in specific procedures can be valuable resources, but they also can create risks of indirect bribes.

By way of illustration, Ralph Lauren Corporation's FCPA action was based on the company's acceptance of responsibility for bribes paid by its agent to customs officials in Argentina over the span of five years. These payments were made to improperly obtain paperwork for customs clearance, permit clearance of items without the necessary paperwork, permit clearance of prohibited items, and avoid customs inspections. The broker submitted invoices to the company with illegitimate line items for "Loading and Delivery Expenses" and "Stamp Tax/Label Tax" to disguise the bribe payments and justify them as proper. The line items contained no backup support. As a result, U.S. enforcement authorities found that Ralph Lauren had failed to conduct proper and effective due diligence on the customs broker, and had failed to detect a single improper payment in the review process for authorization of reimbursement payments to the broker.

THE FCPA IN LATIN AMERICA

Other FCPA actions involving custom officials in Latin America, such as the Ball Corp. case in Argentina, the Helmerich & Payne case in Argentina and Venezuela, and the American Rice case in Haiti, highlight the potential problems associated with moving goods in and out of countries. In the Ball Corp. case, the company's newly acquired Argentine subsidiary paid more than US$106,000 to customs officials in 2006 and 2007 to circumvent the country's byzantine restrictions on importing equipment for use in manufacturing, which eventually cost the company US$300,000 in penalties. Similarly, in the Helmerich & Payne case, from 2004 to 2008 the company's subsidiaries in Argentina and Venezuela bribed customs officials to import and export equipment and materials for operating oil rigs, which led to penalties of US$1.38 million. In the American Rice case, employees paid several bribes in 1998 and 1999 to Haitian customs officials to escape the country's protectionist import taxes on Rice, which led to felony convictions and jail time for two employees.

Companies can manage customs risks in various ways. They can:

➢ Implement systems to verify import or export documentation before it is presented to customs officials. The more accurate the documentation is up front, the less likely officials will find a reason to slow down the process

➢ Use local suppliers as much as possible to reduce the need to ship across international borders, thereby minimizing the need to interact with customs officials in the first place.

> Research entry points to learn which ports are more prone to corruption than others and which customs lanes have officials that are known for requesting payments. Armed with this kind of information, companies can try to route their shipments away from FCPA risks.

> Plan ahead by factoring delays into business plans and maintaining reserves. This relieves some of the pressure on employees to make improper payments, depriving customs agents of timing "leverage."

> Take as a loss any perishable goods that are held up, recognizing that this strategy can reduce future bribery requests. Often times, once a company establishes that it will not give into pressures to bribe, the next customs entry will go much smoother.

> Internalize the work that would otherwise be conducted by a customs broker, bringing in-house the work that third parties would do.

> Reinforce the nature of customs-related risk in anti-corruption training and communications.

> Implement monitoring mechanisms for customs transactions in high-risk markets.

In general, compliance officers should be alert to circumstances—such as a surge in shipping delays—that may cause a temporary spike in FCPA risks. Even when compliance measures put the company at a temporary disadvantage related to customs clearance and entry, they are essential to managing one of Latin America's highest areas of corruption risk.

Police and Extortion

In some parts of Latin America, police present chronic corruption risk for companies and their employees. Typical examples are the municipal checkpoint on the Venezuelan highway, where officers commonly won't allow a company's truck to pass unless the driver makes an "unofficial" payment, or when a Mexican police officer impounds the company car and will not release it without payment of a "fee." It is not surprising that, in the 2016 Latin America Corruption Survey, 82% of Mexican respondents describe the level of corruption associated with Mexican police as "significant."

Some legitimate extortion payments can constitute exceptions to the FCPA's wide-ranging prohibition on payments made to influence government officials. Payments made based on imminent threats to health and safety, for example, would not constitute FCPA violations. If an official holds a gun to an employee's head or is about to poke the employee with a dirty needle at immigration, bribe payments could be warranted – and permissible.

Problems occur when companies try to stretch this exception to other types of threats. In particular, commercial necessity does not trigger the exception. Holding goods in the police yard unless an employee pays a bribe would not qualify. Therefore, companies should consider suspect all explanations of economic coercion. The rule of thumb dictated by U.S. enforcement officials is whether the payer could have turned his or her back and walked away.

To respond to police risk in Latin America, companies can develop various strategies:

> Learn the local terminology for corruption. Knowing words like *mordida* ("a bite") in Mexico and *propina* ("a tip") in Brazil, both of which are terms to mean bribery, will help companies track and identify issues when they occur and train teams to avoid them.

> When training employees, use role-playing scenarios that include examples of petty corruption. What do you do, let's say, when a police officer pulls you over and refuses to let you go without a payment?

> Do not give police a reason to pull over company vehicles. Companies can make sure, for example, that licenses and registrations are updated, taillights are working, and drivers are properly trained on road safety rules.

> Have communication mechanisms in place so employees can seek compliance feedback in real time when issues arise. Drivers can carry the cell phone numbers of a local compliance officer to be called in cases of emergencies.

> Spend extra time during compliance audits reviewing transactions related to police, such as with petty cash disbursements.

> Use the FCPA as a shield. When a police officer makes a bribe request, for example, an acceptable response by the employee

could be, "I don't mean to be rude, but I simply cannot make the payment, or I'd lose my job."

➤ Be ready to wait. Delays often are the corrupt official's best friend. The police officer might make an employee wait at a checkpoint until he decides to finally let you go.

Strategies like these can help companies mitigate corruption risks before they surface, and deal with them when they do.

Gifts and Hospitality

Gifts and hospitality present some of the thorniest issues for companies. In most countries in Latin America, business is often conducted in social settings, and thus developing personal relationships is key. Paying for lunch or tickets to a sporting event might be a basic expectation, but what happens when the recipient is a public official? A company might want to fly a foreign client who happens to work for a state-owned entity to its headquarters to show off its new technology. It might want to use tickets to an event to build goodwill or increase visibility in the eyes of that client. It might choose to give a gift as a gesture of hospitality.

The FCPA does not prohibit providing gifts or hospitality to foreign officials. In 1988, the U.S. Congress amended the FCPA to include an affirmative defense for "reasonable and *bona fide*" expenditures involving foreign officials, "such as travel and lodging expenses." The amendment stipulates that the expenses must be "directly related" to "the promotion, demonstration, or explanation of products or services; or the execution or performance of a contract with a foreign government or agency thereof." Even though the amendment specifically mentions travel and lodging, its coverage can be interpreted to extend to other forms of hospitality as well, insofar as they are for the promotion, demonstration, and explanation of products or services or the execution of a contract.

Certain FCPA cases, however, highlight that these practices are high risk and should be conducted with great care and attention to compliance. For example, the insurance company Aon paid US$16.2 million in penalties after the company's Costa Rican subsidiary treated executives from the government-owned reinsurance company to "educational" conferences, with no clear business purpose, in Cairo, Cologne, Monte Carlo, Munich, London, Paris, and Zurich. Similarly, the aircraft maintenance company Dallas Airmotive paid US$14 million in penalties after the company, among other things, treated a sergeant in the Brazilian Air Force and his wife to a paid vacation.

To ensure compliance with the FCPA, a company's gift giving should be conducted pursuant to a company-wide compliance policy. Companies often set specific value and frequency caps that require internal management approvals. Policies restrict gifts to those of nominal values because, ultimately, a gift with a low value is less likely to influence an official to take a specific action to further the giver's business. Companies should avoid allowing employees to give or receive lavish gifts, like sports cars, jewelry, and golf memberships. Giving cash or cash equivalents should also be prohibited. Companies' policies sometimes require that gifts carry a company's logo, underscoring the fact that the gift is meant to increase corporate visibility and reputation, not to improperly influence a specific act. Gifts should never be permitted in response to a request by an official, especially when the company has business pending before the recipient official or when the recipient official is a decision-maker on a matter affecting the company.

Similarly, many companies adopt specific policies to guide meals and entertainment with officials. Perhaps they limit meal expenditures to US$100 per official per meal, with the possibility of obtaining approvals for higher values that are reasonable given the context of the situation. Entertainment might have cumulative value caps for a year, or caps on the numbers of times an official can be entertained. Policies usually prohibit excessive expenditures on alcohol and all expenditures on lewd entertainment. The donor should be present when the entertainment is provided. Travel should never include anything above economy class, unless the official pays.

When reviewing these types of expenditures for compliance, other helpful considerations include:

> **What is the intent?** At its core, the question of whether gifts, travel, and entertainment to foreign officials are consistent with the FCPA's anti-bribery provisions centers around the giver's intent. Is the purpose innocent? Is the offering intended to promote permissible acts, such as general goodwill and reputation? Is there a legitimate business reason for the travel, such as the need to educate the official about a new product,

or does the offering serve as part of an impermissible *quid pro quo* between the giver and the foreign official? Is it corrupt, done for the specific purpose of obtaining or retaining business or improperly influencing the official?

> **Is the activity transparent?** The more that a gift, travel, or entertainment is provided openly, the less likely that the giver will be deemed to have corrupt intent. Corruption is an activity that is normally conducted in secret. Transparency helps establish legitimacy, meaning that companies should keep detailed internal records about the activity that can be produced to outside parties if needed. They should, where appropriate, disclose to the outside world the ways in which they choose to promote goodwill and build their reputations.

> **Is the activity consistent with local foreign law and custom?** If it is not, it could signal to U.S. enforcement officials that the giver is acting with corrupt intent.

> **Is the activity adequately recorded and tracked?** Companies should maintain specific information like the name and title of the official, the business relationship with the official, the value and cost of the benefit provided, the number of gifts, travel, and entertainment provided to the official in the last year, the business purpose of the expenditure, the methods of payment, and the name of the company personnel who reviewed and approved the disbursement.

> **Are all facts and circumstances considered in the review?** Enforcement officials review expenditures with "20/20 vision." They consider all facts and circumstances related to an issue. Companies should, too. For example, patterns of giving to the

same official, the nature of the company's business currently before the official or that might soon come before the official, or a particular government agency's tainted reputation are all factors that could change an analysis. The picture in retrospect might even include events that had not yet happened at the moment the activity took place.

The fact that relationships and social interactions play a major role in business in some parts of Latin America means that companies will often see a legitimate need to give gifts and hospitality to officials. When done in a controlled way, this activity can be compliant with international anti-corruption norms.

Facilitating Payments

Some officials in Latin America—whether they be regulatory officials, customs officials, police officers, or others—can have a tendency to justify "small" payment requests as legitimate "grease" payments. Payers might also excuse them as minimal and insignificant. Indeed, there are some circumstances in which these types of payments can be legally permissible as "facilitating payments" under the FCPA's anti-bribery provisions. But the exception is quite limited. To qualify, a payment must be made to expedite or secure a "routine government action," and the official action must be non-discretionary (*i.e.*, the official must have no legal basis to refuse to provide the service).

The lack of statutory specificity seems to encourage creative interpretations of the facilitating payments exception. It is not uncommon to hear someone in the region describe a larger payment, perhaps a US$15,000 customs payment or a US$9,000 immigration payment, as a permissible facilitating payment, when they clearly are not. While no statutory value limit on facilitating payments exists, it would be difficult in practice to justify any significant payment, such as in the hundreds of dollars, as "facilitating."

If a company's employees make such payments, the payments should be vetted and approved by a compliance officer, and should be properly and openly recorded in the company's books. Compliance officials should be careful to point out to employees that any sizeable payment, even one that might arguably fit within the exception, can invite the scrutiny of enforcement officials. This means that, even if a company were to prevail in its view that a large payment qualifies for the exception, victory would come only after the disruption and expense of a formal investigation. Moreover, other international anti-corruption laws, like the U.K. Bribery Act ("UKBA"), still prohibit facilitating payments and might be implicated. In Brazil, for example, such payments can subject companies to civil and administrative liability, and can subject individuals to imprisonment of up to 12 years and a fine.

Misconceptions about facilitating payments also frequently lead to questions about materiality of payment values under the FCPA. In fact, no materiality threshold for an FCPA violation exists. FCPA actions have been built on a series of smaller payments that, in the aggregate, amount to significant expenditures. This can include not only monetary payments, but also other things of value, like gifts and entertainment. For example, Diageo gave rice cakes and other gifts to government officials in South Korea, and other countries, ranging in value from US$100 to US$300 per recipient that, in the aggregate, amounted to US$64,184 over four years. This, in part, made up the basis for its FCPA enforcement action. In another series of ongoing FCPA investigations—the so-called "princeling" investigations—the activities of various banks in China do not appear to deal with specific monetary payments. Instead, the investigations focus on firms that provided jobs to children of high-ranking Chinese officials.

Even if it is true that authorities are less likely to prosecute companies for individual smaller payments, companies should still focus on preventing them. If FCPA authorities were to detect smaller payments, they might initiate wider investigations to determine whether those small issues are actually systemic. These wider investigations, in themselves, can be costly and disruptive for a company. Thus, by assuming that authorities are only interested in large payments, companies run the risk of ignoring the full picture.

Compliance officers should ask questions about any payments described as "facilitating payments" and make sure the activity, if it occurs, is subject to strict oversight.

Family-Owned Businesses and Acquisitions

Family-owned businesses are common in Latin America. A 2014 study conducted by Ernst and Young concluded that 85% of the companies in the region are family-owned, generating 60% of Latin America's GDP and 70% of the workforce in Latin America and the Caribbean. This can be explained in part by structural factors, like the relative weakness of local laws designed to protect minority shareholder rights, which makes it difficult for family companies to attract outside investors.

The prevalence of family ownership is highly relevant to managing corruption risk. Frequently, foreigners investing in the region will find themselves partnering with homegrown companies that lack common accounting standards, corporate governance transparency, or basic internal controls. This can complicate the ability of outsiders to perform the type of anti-corruption due diligence necessary to manage corruption risks in mergers and acquisitions.

In particular, companies can be liable for ongoing corrupt acts of the companies they purchase, as well as pre-acquisition violations in some circumstances based on a theory of successor liability. FCPA enforcers see the purchaser as acquiring not only the target company's assets but its liabilities as well. This means that, if the purchaser could have uncovered the target's FCPA violations through reasonable due diligence and fails to do so, it is considered to have inherited that liability. FCPA enforcers most certainly will hold the acquirer responsible for any ongoing corrupt acts that take place after closing.

Complicating matters is when local companies are offended at the prospect of having to be vetted for corruption issues, leading to pushback on due diligence, even if the family has nothing to hide. The family might be reluctant to open up its books and operations to outside lawyers and accountants. As a result, those negotiating the deal might need to factor in time to explain why anti-corruption due diligence is necessary as an evolving business requirement of international work. Even if they gain access to a company's records, purchasers might not have a full understanding of the company's entire history and details of its business operations.

In these transactions, the need to know the real value of the targeted entity may be just as important to a purchaser as potential FCPA liability is. If the target has built its business on corrupt acts, the only way to accurately assign a value to the company is by knowing about those acts and factoring the associated liabilities into the target's value.

In practice, purchasers lower acquisition prices when they uncover corruption liabilities. A company might still choose to proceed with the acquisition despite identifying FCPA issues. It might disclose the findings to U.S. authorities. At the very least, it should remediate the issues after closing. This can include terminating responsible employees, implementing heightened controls in areas of prior weakness, and quickly training personnel in high-risk areas.

Latin American companies with hopes of being acquired are learning that they, too, can increase value and minimize potential FCPA roadblocks by implementing anti-corruption compliance programs early on. Without a program in place, the seller should expect the possibility of major headaches as the deal progresses.

Monopolies and Compliance Risk

In many Latin American countries, monopolies can be common. Unfortunately, these political connections present common FCPA compliance challenges for companies doing business there because they often facilitate, and are reinforced by, practices like self-dealing, nepotism, and influence-peddling. For example, Mexico's history has been colored by a handful of companies gaining entrenched power in sectors like media and communications.

At its core, the prevalence of monopolies creates problems related to market power. Foreign companies find themselves negotiating with the only game in town. When a company needs the monopoly partner much more than the partner needs the company, it can be difficult to impose compliance assurances as part of the company's third-party due diligence process. It might not even be able to open up lines of communication with the company's ultimate beneficial owners, the ones who might need to give such assurances. This is because, over generations, the family members might have grown so disconnected from the company's management that they are difficult to reach. At the same time, compliance conditions can be essential given the risk that a monopoly could make improper payments on the company's behalf.

Data reinforces the popular perception that a small elite dom-
inates both business and politics in the region, which increases the
risk of monopolies. According to World Bank data from 2010 to 2014,
Latin American countries' Gini coefficients averaged 0.48, which
is higher than the coefficients for Africa (0.42), North American
(0.37), Asia (0.36), Europe (0.30), and the world as a whole (0.38).
The Gini coefficient is a common measure of income equality, where
a perfectly equal society would receive a score of 0 and society where
one individual earned an entire country's GDP would earn a score
of 1. Therefore, it is not surprising that a Pew Research Center poll
in 2014 found that an average of 73% of Latin Americans in polled
countries believed that the wealthy had too much power in their
country—a number higher than for any other continent. In these
places, monopolies often are run by politically connected elites who
move back and forth between government and business. A father
might own a conglomerate, and his son might be a senator.

Companies investing in Latin America can take various steps
to manage these situations:

> **Understand risks and recognize red flags associated with
monopolies.** This includes gaining information on the
monopoly's ownership, its relationship with government officials, and its business reputation. A monopoly's refusal to
sign an anti-corruption compliance certification should raise
concerns.

> **Use local actors, trained in compliance, to interface with
monopolies.** Monopolies often will be more responsive when
engaged by locals, because they are more apt to trust those

who are familiar to them—such as a salesperson in the region where the monopoly is based, or a third-party agent with local know-how. Additionally, locals can better navigate otherwise complicated systems, including arranging meetings with hard-to-reach owners, and they can better understand negotiation cues. Local representatives, however, should also be fully trained on FCPA risks and anti-corruption compliance expectations in order to serve as a company's best spokespeople for compliance.

➢ **Work with competitors to level the playing field.** Some sectors have begun to establish collective action strategies for compliance. In Latin America, for example, several energy companies have signed a formal collective action agreement in which they have committed publicly to conducting all business operations in a fair, honest, and transparent manner, and to enhance integrity and transparency in their global day-to-day business operations. At the core of this agreement is a pledge not to pay or accept bribes. In situations like this, when a monopoly deals with customers who have entered into an integrity pact, it might have no choice but to embrace compliance standards. This activity also has risks, as communications between competitors must be conducted in a way that does not run afoul of anti-trust and competition rules. Such risks can be addressed up front to avoid any actual or apparent impropriety.

➢ **Be willing to escalate an issue.** If a company confronts a monopoly that is unwilling to cooperate on compliance, shows signs of public corruption, or demands commercial bribes itself, the company should consider escalating these issues. It might choose to share its information with local, national, or federal authorities, or engage chambers of commerce. Depending on the situation, such action can help establish new avenues for doing business in a compliant way. These steps should be conducted with appropriate counsel so that any associated risks are fully understood.

➤ **Be willing to walk away.** If the risks of partnering with a monopoly seem too high, a company should not be afraid to walk from the opportunity. This could mean missing promising business possibilities. Then again, given the risks of FCPA non-compliance, that might be the wisest decision to make.

Finally, many monopolies themselves are integrated into the global economy and are beginning to feel the pressures of compliance expectations. To obtain loans, attract investment, or do global deals, more and more they are expected to demonstrate strong compliance practices as well. This dynamic can help facilitate investors' compliance efforts as well.

Risks When Bubbles Burst

Boom and bust cycles are common in Latin America. The region on the whole is known for periods of economic expansion followed by precipitous collapse. In the 1970s, increased commodity prices led to economic growth that ended abruptly in the 1980s, triggering a sharp debt crisis. In the early 1990s, market-oriented reforms created a surge in short-term capital that ended, again abruptly, in the Tequila crisis of 1994. Currently, Brazil faces economic contraction after years of impressive growth. Some speculate wider implications for the region.

Given this history and these cycles, companies should keep in mind that corruption risks are affected when economies contract. For example, companies might feel more pressure to cut corners when business environments worsen. When economies implode, it can be difficult for multinational companies to exit, especially those that have invested millions in new plants, distribution infrastructures, and other fixed assets. They will usually be forced to compete for fewer and choosier private sector customers, as well as a reduced number of publicly funded projects. This puts more pressure on sales personnel to hit targets and show results. The temptation to do whatever is necessary to stay ahead, or stay employed, increases. These pressures increase the risks that staff and agents of multinationals will resort to bribe payments. Companies might also confront more aggressive bribe demands when markets fall, which create a smaller amount of public resources that corrupt officials can leverage to benefit personally, leading some officials who may be inclined to act with corrupt intent to be more forceful with their demands.

Sometimes a contracting economy results in public dissatisfaction that can bring new parties and personalities to power. These new leaders might be motivated to uncover bribery schemes involving their predecessors, because making previous administrations look bad can bolster their own standing. Foreign companies representing limited local constituencies are obvious targets for increased scrutiny and blame. Such shifts in political power effectively mean that companies engaged in wrongdoing stand a greater risk of being caught when economies decline. They may even face greater likelihood of enforcement in the United States if a country's new leadership is more willing to share evidence with U.S. authorities.

New leaders might be more corrupt than prior ones. They might choose to extort money from companies, perhaps by threatening license revocation, increased taxes, or audits. If an unscrupulous company already has government contracts in place that are based on bribe payments, new governments might seek new bribes to keep them. Take Siemens Argentina as an example, which won a US$1 billion national identity card contract from the Carlos Menem administration by bribing government officials at a time when the Argentine economy appeared strong. The economy then fell into crisis, and President Menem lost his bid for a third term. In 1999, the new administration of President Fernando De la Rúa threatened to terminate Siemens' contract, unless the company paid more bribes. Circumstances like this highlight not only why it is a bad idea for companies to engage in corruption in the first place, but also how a situation can quickly worsen when local economic conditions change.

In some cases, such as what has been witnessed in Argentina and Venezuela in the last several years, governments choose to take more active roles in the market when economies decline. They modify regulations, create export taxes, implement price and currency controls, and take other actions to keep the economy from slipping further. In extreme cases, they nationalize companies and industries. When these changes occur, the entire legal underpinnings of a company's investment in a country can change. As a result, companies find themselves forced to interact with officials in ways they had never done before, increasing opportunities for bribe requests.

What may be the most pernicious result of boom and bust cycles is the effect they have on the poor and middle classes. They often result in greater gaps in distribution of wealth within societies. In turn, the more inequality that exists between social classes, the more opportunity for corruption to grow institutionalized. This is because some are left with a smaller stake in society while others are positioned to concentrate and consolidate their power. This creates conditions allowing for greater government capture and impunity. Inequality impedes economic growth, which can further drive those in power to seek to secure sources of personal enrichment, creating a vicious cycle.

— —

Latin America overall has an average CPI score of 37, which is about 50th percentile for the world as a whole. This puts the region at about the same level of perceived corruption as China or India— about 10 points behind Greece and Ghana and about 10 points ahead of Russia and Iran. A simple average of the region's corruption scores suggests that the region has made some progress over the past decade, with scores increasing about 9.5%. However, a weighted average that takes into account the size of each country's GDP shows no progress in the region over the past 10 years, and a weighted average accounting for population shows a slight rise in perceived corruption risk of less than 2%. Thus, large economies whose perceived corruption has risen—such as Brazil, Colombia, Mexico, or Venezuela—seem to overwhelm smaller economies that have seen some progress—such as Bolivia, Costa Rica, Cuba, El Salvador, Ecuador, Nicaragua, Panama, Paraguay, and Uruguay. Against this general backdrop, it is also useful to examine Latin American countries individually, discussed next in Chapter 3.

Chapter 3

Specific Corruption Risks in Key Latin American Markets

Empirical data and FCPA enforcement history reveal some common corruption risks that companies tend to confront in certain key Latin American markets, including Argentina, Brazil, Chile, Colombia, Mexico, Peru, and Venezuela. Though these are generalizations, they still serve to establish starting points for companies attempting to assess risks when doing business in the region. Depending on a company's sector or industry, some of these guiding points will be more relevant than others. Additional risks might be at play, too.

The following summaries can help convey a general impression about the nature of risks usually confronted in these important markets.

Argentina: Corruption Risks on the Río de la Plata

Former President Carlos Menem was known to drive a red Ferrari while he led Argentina in the 1990s. In response to criticism, he said, "I am going to leave this car as property of the nation, but, meanwhile, I shall use it myself." His popularity remained strong. Indeed, Argentines are known to complain about corruption in their country, while at the same time appearing to have a certain level of toleration. A common saying in the region is that, "Argentina is the country of the future, and it will always be."

At the very least, Argentina has not found a way to counter the sense of impunity among its public leaders, which is reflected in data from Transparency International and the World Bank. Argentina scored 32 in the 2015 CPI, putting the country at about 36th percentile worldwide. Similarly, Argentina came in at about 40th percentile for the World Bank's controls for corruption score, which measures the actions countries take to stop corruption. Fortunately, the country has improved its CPI and controls of corruption scores significantly since 2002— by about 14% and 11% respectively, although there is still much room for improvement. Despite increasing its absolute CPI score, Argentina has actually fallen in the relative rankings from 70th in 2002 to 107th in 2015. Moreover, the country has also long received low scores from the World Bank for regulatory quality, suggesting that the country's laws are opaque and unclear enough to create corruption risk.

Prominent areas of corruption risk in Argentina include the following:

Customs. Argentina has a bad reputation for corruption among its customs officials. In an FCPA action against Ralph Lauren Corporation, the company's Argentine subsidiary paid customs officials through a third-party broker to improperly obtain or facilitate customs clearance. In the 2011 Ball Corp. FCPA action, the company's Argentine subsidiary was alleged to have paid more than US$100,000 in bribes to import prohibited equipment and parts. Making matters worse, Argentina recently had a program of stiff tariffs on exports, creating yet another opportunity for customs officials to seek undue payments.

Corruption in Argentina's customs system severely affects not only multinational companies but also local companies whose businesses rely on imports. One method adopted by local lawyers to mitigate customs-related risk is to advise clients to expect a six-month delay for customs clearance, which generally is a longer timeframe than customs officials will hold up a shipment while seeking a bribe. The delays accepted by this approach suggest just how difficult it is to work with Argentine customs without paying bribes.

Shell Companies. Corrupt schemes in Argentina are often carried out using *empresas fantasmas* (literally, "ghost companies"), which are phantom companies set up within Argentina or offshore to hide or improperly channel funds. For example, Siemens used the "Argentine Consulting Group" without an apparent business justification, other than to transfer funds back to government officials, who created one of various bases for its blockbuster FCPA penalty.

In 2012, the tax collection authority in the country closed down more than 300,000 shell companies suspected of operating for purposes of tax evasion. Given the prevalence of these schemes, any use of third-party agents, brokers, or consultants in Argentina should be subject to heightened scrutiny, including robust due diligence and ongoing monitoring.

Currency controls. Beginning in 2011, in an effort to stem capital flight, Argentina began implementing severe restrictions on the ability of businesses and individuals to convert pesos into dollars. This led to the proliferation of an overt black market for dollars, where exchange rates at times have exceeded the country's official rate by more than three-fold. These developments create incentives for companies to engage in opaque and risky payment structures to reduce risk that their profits will be stuck in currency with uncertain value. Efforts to "work around" exchange controls also implicate anti-money laundering laws as well as the FCPA's books and records and internal controls provisions.

Dramatic policy swings. Economic policy in Argentina tends to color corruption risk. Over the years, it has swung between extremes, moving from International Monetary Fund-backed, market-oriented privatizations to nationalizations and *dirigisme*, which is a state-centralized form of managing a country's economy. Each extreme brings with it different corruption risks. For example, poorly managed privatizations in the 1990s resulted in huge sums of money flowing into officials' private bank accounts instead of public coffers. Under the Kirchner Administration, the government established just the opposite— widespread interference in the economy, creating different forms of government interaction related to price controls, nationalizations (like that of Argentine oil and gas exploration company YPF), and cost reporting requirements in highly sensitive industries, like agriculture and energy. Such rapid and dramatic changes create confusion within institutions and the sectors they regulate. They leave government institutions weakened and more vulnerable to corruption.

Capitalism among friends. *Capitalismo de amigos* ("capitalism among friends") is a common phrase in Argentina, reflecting a tendency of government officials to direct business to entities with which they are personally related. This creates heightened corruption risk in public procurement. For example, President Kirchner was accused of directing public contracts to a businessman from her native Santa Cruz Province who, in turn, booked hotels owned by the Kirchner family for rooms that were never used.

Brazil: A Time of Dramatic Anti-Corruption Developments

The dramatic developments related to corruption over the last several years in Brazil, including the adoption of the Brazilian Clean Companies Act, underscore a period of rapid change for a country known for high corruption risk. To add to the upheaval, the Brazilian authorities' investigation of Petrobras continues to expand. The Petrobras investigation is now turning many businesses in the country upside down, implicating dozens of companies and numerous high-levels political officials.

All these anti-corruption developments have occurred during a period of vast economic transition. For years, Brazil experienced significant foreign direct investment ("FDI"). According to the United Nations Conference on Trade and Development, Brazil made up the sixth largest destination for global FDI in 2013. New FDI into Brazil reached US$64 billion in 2013. By the end of 2015, prosperity had turned to sluggishness, with an economy facing serious contraction. After years of investment grade status, in 2015 Standard & Poor's and Fitch Ratings both downgraded the country's status to junk. These dramatic sways have the potential of generating new and varying corruption threats.

Below are five risk areas that companies should watch out for:

Sophisticated corruption. Brazil is not a "Banana Republic," to borrow the pejorative term sometimes used to describe underdeveloped Latin American economies that have traditionally been dependent on the U.S. economy. Nor is it the highly mature and developed economy of a country like, say, Canada. Brazil is a unique mix. It has a large, sophisticated, and modern private sector and relatively weak government institutions. Returns on investment at times can be impressive, as are poverty rates and infrastructure gaps. When U.S. and other companies enter the Brazilian market, they should expect to encounter a sophisticated and savvy business sector. Corruption schemes are also sophisticated. They should be alert for, and have a strategy to avoid, large and complex bribery schemes—such as price fixing and collusion with competitors and elaborate manipulation of public bids using multiple parties.

Complex and unique regulatory regimes. Brazil is an elaborately regulated country. In a 2014 report on paying taxes worldwide, the professional services firm PricewaterhouseCoopers found that it, took an average company 2,600 person hours per year to comply with the Brazilian tax code, making the country's taxes the most time-consuming in the world. (For comparison's sake, an average company in the United States required only 175 hours per year to comply with taxes.) Intricate rules in areas like tax and environmental regulations and public procurement create room to disguise improper payments. They also create opportunity for FCPA books and records violations. Engaging the help of local counsel to better understand these rules, so that companies can determine whether or not regulatory-related payments are indeed proper, may be necessary.

Personal relationships. In Brazil, personal and professional relationships oftentimes are intricately intertwined. Thus, before talking business with potential clients or business partners in Brazil, it is often necessary to form connections with them on a personal level first—to talk sports, family, music, or any other subject that makes them feel at ease. This is the way to get things done in Brazil, and these close relationships can sometimes eventually facilitate the formation of illicit schemes. Furthermore, when doing due diligence or investigative work in Brazil, transactions under review are at times better understood when one considers the personal relationships behind them.

"Jeitinho brasileiro." The phrase *jeitinho brasileiro* (the "Brazilian Way") is as much an attitude as an act. It refers to the grace by which Brazilians handle situations, accomplish tasks, or find paths around problems. It is what makes the world love the country—what gives innovative rhythm to bossa nova, what inspires Brazilian soccer with improvisation, and what makes Brazilians such fun-loving people. In the context of international business, however, the *jeitinho brasileiro* can also mean the "Brazilian Work Around." Companies working in Brazil should be aware of this dynamic. Local agents might repeatedly tell a company one thing, and then just as easily and gracefully do another. Such dynamics heighten the need to implement robust reporting requirements and internal controls, and to consistently monitor operations.

Political parties. The deep involvement of Brazilian political parties in local corruption schemes became evident in the Petrobras investigations. Kickback schemes related to Petrobras and other companies not only involved self-enrichment of government officials who, in turn, used illicit funds in ways such as purchasing luxury art and exotic cars. Illicit funds were also channeled to support political parties and campaigns. Perceptions of this form of corruption were apparent in the 2016 Latin America Corruption Survey, where a spectacular 94% of Brazilian respondents described "significant" corruption in local political parties.

Chile: Understanding Local Law, Enforcement, and Deterrence

By most measures, Chile generally is considered low risk for corruption issues. The country has earned the best CPI scores in Latin America every year since the Index was launched in 1996. In fact, Chile regularly ranks on par with the United States, although it still falls significantly behind anti-corruption powerhouses such as Denmark, Finland, and New Zealand.

Chile's regulatory processes are also considered sound, and the application of its laws reliable. This established degree of rule of law is probably the most relevant corruption risk indicator for companies doing business there. While many other countries in Latin America experience low levels of local law deterrence, in Chile deterrence is on full display. In fact, companies operating there need to worry not only about the FCPA but about enforcement of local corruption laws as well. Of note, in 2013, Chile sentenced three executives from the agrobusiness Sociedad Agrícolas Mecanizado Ltda to jail time and penalties of US$63,000 for bribery involving water rights. The same year, the Chilean prosecutor's office granted a *suspensión condicional* ("conditional suspension")—analogous to an SEC settlement or a DOJ deferred prosecution agreement —obliging the paint and dye company Industrias Ceresita to pay US$2.5 million to the community where it had built a paint factory with corrupt licenses. As of 2015, Chilean prosecutors had charged owners and executives from the large financial group Grupo Penta with tax fraud, bribery, and money laundering in connection with an alleged scheme to provide financial contributions to the Chilean right-wing party Independent Democratic Union during the 2012 elections. Thus, to manage risks in Chile, it is important for companies to understand relevant aspects of its local anti-corruption framework.

Below are three key components of the local legal regime:

Corporate criminal liability. While other countries in the region—such as Brazil, Argentina, and Peru—have been resistant to establish criminal liability for the corrupt acts of legal persons, Chile has embraced it. In 2009, for example, Chile's Congress passed the Corporate Criminal Liability Law that applies to money laundering, the financing of terrorism, and bribery of domestic and foreign public officials.

That is not to say, however, that the establishment of corporate criminal liability came about easily. In Chile, like in many civil law jurisdictions throughout the region, many reject the notion that companies can form the *mens rea* necessary to commit willful acts. But a strong political will arose in 2009 to join OECD's Anti-Bribery Convention and satisfy its requirements, which included establishing corporate liability for corrupt acts. Even a representative of Chile's Production and Commerce Federation testified about that organization's support to Congress, "I affirm that it is unquestionable that in the modern and globalized world, regulations should develop and confront new realities. The existence of criminal figures like the ones that this legislation addresses is grave and should be addressed with force because, if not, the development of our societies and well-being will be harmed." This view contrasts the business pushback that similar legislation has triggered in countries like Brazil and Peru.

Interestingly, in the case of bribery, Chilean law does not attribute criminal liability to legal entities based on a theory that the company has willfully performed the criminal act. Instead, it generally applies a theory that the corporate entity failed to implement and fulfill its obligation of preventing the specific crime.

Compliance program certifications. Chile's Corporate Criminal Liability Law explicitly provides credit for corporate compliance programs (*modelos de prevención*). Since corporate entities are obligated to prevent specific crimes like bribery, one way they can fulfill this obligation is by implementing a compliance program.

Chile's approach to anti-corruption compliance is unique because the Corporate Criminal Liability Law provides that corporate entities can have their compliance programs certified. Local firms, authorized under Chile's Securities and Insurance Authority, are tasked with reviewing companies' compliance programs and certifying them as sufficient. Firms that have been authorized to certify compliance programs are listed on the Authority's website, which additionally lists companies that already have been certified.

Compliance program certification is still subject to some debate in Chile. Some maintain that certifications should entitle a company to full immunity. Others think that obtaining a certification merely increases the standard of proof in the case of a violation. The government would have the burden of establishing that the company did not fulfill its obligation to prevent the crime, despite having implemented and obtaining certification for its compliance program. What is clear is that, when companies do not have such certificates, they have a harder time demonstrating that they have fulfilled their obligations.

Leniency agreements. Chilean law provides for Conditional Suspensions of Proceedings that can occur during investigations. They amount to settlements between prosecutors and defendants. Courts approve the settlements and determine conditions that must be met within a defined period of time for defendants to be acquitted. Conditions can include adoption of a compliance program, obligations to make restitution payments, or other requirements. For example, in April 2014, Chilean authorities secured a US$2.5 million settlement with Chile's Industrias Ceresita for alleged bribe payments to public officials in connection with construction permits for industrial premises. The settlement involved numerous conditions, including making major infrastructure improvements in the affected municipality and even painting the facades of the buildings that face the main squares of the town, a creative resolution for a paint and dye company.

Colombia: Legacy Risks During A Quiet Boom

Colombia has been quietly boomi ʾɡ According to the World Bank and the IMF, Colombia is Latin America's fourth largest economy and the fastest growing of the region's largest economies, with a predicted growth rate of between four and five percent for the next several years. Companies and businesspeople from neighboring and troubled Venezuela continue to flock to the Colombian cities of Bogotá, Cartagena, and Barranquilla for opportunities. The activities of the Revolutionary Armed Forces of Colombia (FARC) have subsided.

On the anti-corruption front, the country has joined the OECD Anti-Bribery Convention. In 2011, the government of Colombia revamped a key corruption law (the *Estatuto Nacional Anticorrupción*). At the conclusion of 2015, Congress approved a foreign bribery law. Recent prosecution efforts have resulted in the imprisonment of the former Mayor of Bogotá and the Governor of Cundinamarca State for corruption-related offenses.

Colombia's economy is still risky. The country earned a score of 37 in the 2015 CPI, which puts it at about 46th percentile worldwide. Furthermore, Colombia's CPI score has remained approximately the same for the past ten years, while the country's World Bank score for controls of corruption has slipped from above median to below average over the last decade. Fortunately, the country has earned high scores from the World Bank for regulatory quality, with significant progress over the last decade.

In Colombia, as in most Latin American countries, public procurements, customs processes, and local regulatory requirements create persistent corruption risks. The following are some other issues that companies should be on alert to:

Narco-terrorism's effects. Colombia's business community has suffered through a long history of bombings, kidnappings, and targeted murders linked to the narcotics trade. The country's security situation has improved dramatically in the last fifteen years, and security threats are now generally limited to rural areas. Nevertheless, compliance officers should be prepared to discuss how to address corruption when personal security may be at risk.

In addition, though drug-related violence has waned, Colombia still has a large and powerful drug industry. The profits from these operations find their ways into the general economy, creating significant money-laundering risks. Drug profits also affect politics, both through corruption and by funding efforts to shape regulations and policies. With these issues in mind, companies should conduct thorough due diligence on counterparties and business associates.

Interactions with the military. Companies operating in rural areas—such as energy and mining companies conducting resource explorations or telecommunications companies building towers—are subject to increased security risks. To address this, some companies partner with the Colombian military to provide enhanced security. Though such activity does not *per se* violate the FCPA, whenever companies pass funds directly to the government, they are increasing their risk of actual and perceived corruption. Companies should apply additional protections to such activity by ensuring that (i) arrangements are memorialized in writing, (ii) funds go to a military entity and not to specific individuals, (iii) the activity is legal under local law, (iv) legitimate services are provided in return for expenditures, and (v) other safeguards are put in place as necessary.

Local governments/social investments. Due to a combination of geography and local laws, Colombian municipalities and regions operate with a high degree of autonomy. In addition, tribal leaders may serve public functions that could make them foreign officials under the FCPA.

Colombia's municipalities are thought to present a significant source of corruption because local leaders often expect companies, especially multinational ones, to make social investments as a condition of operating in their area. Companies that do not cooperate may face strikes and roadblocks. While building schools and health clinics does not necessarily violate the FCPA, such projects present significant risks; directed donations to local charities can be smoke-screens for corrupt payments and have resulted in previous FCPA enforcement actions.

Companies should ensure that the social investments are legal under local law, and should use written agreements to memorialize agreements with institutions rather than individuals. Companies should vet recipient organizations to ensure that they are unrelated to local officials or their relatives, and should create oversight mechanisms to ensure that funds are not diverted to leaders' pockets. To the extent possible, companies should coordinate with national governmental entities to mitigate any appearance of impropriety.

Silver linings. In Colombia, one positive consequence of the recognition of money laundering and security risks is that many Colombian companies now have compliance frameworks in place already. Such programs provide an institutional infrastructure that would also support the development of anti-corruption compliance programs.

Mexico: Corruption in a Familiar Market

U.S. companies find Mexico to be an attractive place to do business for a variety of reasons. The country is our neighbor. Its market is vast. The North American Free Trade Agreement ("NAFTA") has intimately linked the two economies such that Mexico represents the United States' second largest export market and its third largest source of imports. Mexico also feels familiar, given that Mexican culture has permeated the United States, and vice versa.

Concerning FCPA compliance, however, it is important not to let familiarity mask what might be happening behind the screens and illusions that can hide true decision-makers and bad actors. Mexico's CPI score has been stuck in the low-to-mid 30s for a decade, putting the country consistently at or below average for the region. Respondents to the 2016 Latin America Corruption Survey rated Mexico as the third most corrupt major economy in the region, behind Venezuela and Brazil. Furthermore, according to the World Bank, Mexico's controls of corruption score has fallen significantly over the last decade. Surveys of hundreds of business executives by FTI Consulting Mexico found that, in 2014, 43% of business leaders said that all levels of government were "equally corrupt," and, in 2015, 76% of respondents said the same thing. In that survey, approximately one in five business leaders in 2015 reported at least one incident in the prior year in which public officials requested money to facilitate or issue paperwork, perform an official function, or participate in or win a public contract. This corruption risk and the volume of U.S.-Mexico transactions have led the country to be the largest source of known FCPA enforcement actions in Latin America.

Companies commonly face the following corruption threats in Mexico:

The police. It is not uncommon for Mexican police officers to quote false highway rules at traffic stops and demand bribes to avoid imprisonment. Nor is it uncommon for an officer to impound a company vehicle unlawfully and demand bribes to have it released. Companies doing business in Mexico should develop plans for reacting to such corruption and should provide employees likely to receive such demands with training and resources.

Security/extortion. Mexico has several security problems ranging from kidnapping by criminals to extortion by government officials. No statutory exception or defense under the FCPA exists for duress or extortion, but the statute's legislative history suggests that such situations are not subject to the FCPA's anti-bribery provisions. This is because, if an individual makes a payment based on extortion, that individual lacks the corrupt intent necessary to satisfy the offense. At the same time, the FCPA's books and records and internal controls provisions might still apply to these transactions. Thus, if employees are forced to pay bribes under duress or through extortion, companies must ensure that those payments are correctly recorded in their books. Companies should also take precautionary steps to avoid such situations in the future.

Companies might even want to obtain opinions from local anti-corruption lawyers that describe the actual security risks involved in their type of work. How can the employee know that the Mexican police officer is really a police officer? What if the officer wrongfully detains the employee and applies trumped-up charges if a payment is not made? These are real risks that should be considered before they happen.

Large-scale procurements. FCPA enforcement actions like Bridgestone highlight the risks inherent in Mexican procurement processes. From 1999 to 2007, Bridgestone's Latin American subsidiary bribed procurement officials from Mexican state-owned oil company Pemex to influence the purchase of marine hose, an industrial product used in offshore drilling rigs. The Mexican market is large, and so are government procurements. When large dollars (or pesos) are at stake, corruption is more likely to occur. Companies participating in large procurements should take special precautions, such as implementing heightened internal controls and targeted training.

Politically linked companies. Mexico has a relatively small elite dominated by powerful families that frequently have members involved in business and some in politics. In the 2002 book *Mexico's Mandarins*, the respected U.S. scholar on Mexican politics, Roderic Ai Camp, meticulously documented known ties of family, friendship, education, and organizations am ₃ 398 carefully selected Mexican elites. Camp found numerous and diverse ties among elites, both within the business world and between individuals categorized as "capitalist" and individuals categorized as "politicians," "intellectuals," "military," and even, to a lesser extent, "clergy."

These close relationships can blur the lines between public and private activity, creating public corruption risk. For example, a politician from a family that owns a bank might require business with his family's bank as the payoff for an official action. The bottom line is that it is important for companies to know the parties with whom they are dealing.

Opaque regulations. Regulations for everything from construction to taxation can be dense in Mexico. The World Bank puts the country in the bottom quartile worldwide for regulatory quality for obtaining electricity and registering property. Local lawyers can help untangle rules to understand which payment requests are legitimate and which ones are not. A company's consistent commitment to compliance can send a steady message to regulators that it is unwilling to participate in bribery.

Ongoing improvements to local law in Mexico hold promise to help address corruption. In 2012, the Mexican Congress did what few thought was possible: it passed a powerful new public procurement anti-corruption law. In 2015, it amended its Constitution and developed a new National Anti-Corruption System. These are not trivial developments for a country with widespread corruption risk.

Peru: The Shadow of Fujimori

When Alberto Fujimori ruled Peru between 1990 and 2000, he brought security and stability to a country known for "Shining Path" terrorism, economic ruin, and runaway inflation. These accomplishments came with a downside: pervasive corruption at the highest levels of government. President Fujimori now sits in prison serving a 25-year sentence for siphoning away public money.

In 2015, Peru earned a CPI score of 36—about average for the region and the world. Both the country's score and rank have lost some ground over the past decade. Furthermore, in a survey conducted in 2012 by Proética, Transparency International's affiliate there, Peruvians cited corruption as their second highest concern, behind security, with almost half stating that it is one of the country's biggest problems. It is perhaps not surprising, therefore, that two other ex-presidents of Peru besides Fujimori are facing corruption-related investigations, suggesting endemic corruption at the very top of country's ruling elite.

Specific corruption areas to watch out for when doing business in Peru include the following:

Lawyers and impunity. Peru has several well-respected law firms, but certain segments of the bar are known for illicit dealings with the judiciary. The court system is overloaded. If lawyers want their cases moved up the docket, they often need to pay. Some call it *La Danza de los Maletines*, literally meaning lawyers dancing around the courts with suitcases full of money in hand. The Proética survey found that 56% of Peruvians think the judiciary is corrupt. A sense of impunity means that bribery is often straightforward, with little need to devise complex schemes. Even if a lawyer is caught, he or she is ultimately unlikely to be punished.

Business community tolerance. Foreigners doing business in Peru sometimes encounter a considerable degree of tolerance for corruption among the business community, or a willingness to look the other way. Some might say this is directly linked to opinions of Fujimori and his legacy. Many in the business community revere the former president for the stability he brought. He is still so popular that his daughter narrowly lost her bid for the presidency in 2011 and again in 2016. These attitudes, in certain situations, can lead business people to view anti-corruption compliance efforts with skepticism, interpreting them as little more than the usual political criticisms. As a result, conversations about managing corruption risk can take on unexpected dimensions.

Unique mining risks. Mining is big business in Peru, accounting for the majority of the country's exports. Permitting processes are relatively transparent, and government officials working on concessions are generally professional and technically knowledgeable, though corruption risks still exist. Other aspects of the industry can present bigger risks. To obtain exploration and mining rights in some areas of the country, companies need to establish agreements with local indigenous groups. Under local law, these groups have rights to use surface lands in some mining-rich areas of the country. Companies obtain permission to use lands through rent payments, charitable donations, and other benefits. These interactions create risks that companies will give improper payments to local officials to win indigenous support or to circumvent its authority.

Industries with limited licensing. Some industries—such as oil and gas, construction, fishing, and lumber—have more limited granting of licenses and concessions than mining, given the nature of the country's regulatory regime. This results in high levels of competition and pressure to win contracts, giving authorities leverage to extract concessions, creating bribery risk. Procurement officials are known to tell bidders, "no proposal is perfect," implying that bid mistakes can be cured with favors. Bidders might be encouraged to use unscrupulous third-party *operadores* ("operators") in tenders. In particular, the construction sector is known for its cartels. Similarly, lumber quotas in the Amazon create incentives for companies harvesting wood to pay off inspectors to turn a blind eye.

Police. The police force in Peru is one of the most corrupt in the region. Proética reports that, in 2011 and 2012, more than 6,000 police officers were being investigated for corruption. In 2013, the Peruvian authorities initiated the rotation of 80% of the force to disrupt police involvement in criminal activity.

Venezuela: Corruption Risk in Political and Economic Chaos

Hugo Chavez came to power in Venezuela in 1999, riding a wave of dissatisfaction with the corrupt oligarchic elite that had governed the country for years. Despite his promise, corruption in Venezuela seems to have only grown worse. In fact, the country's CPI score has fallen 32% since 2002, which means the country has fallen from about 20th percentile in the world to about 5th. Only Haiti's perceived corruption rivals Venezuela's among Latin American countries. Respondents to the 2016 Latin America Corruption Survey found Venezuela to be the most corrupt country in the region (Haiti was not surveyed). Perceptions of corruption in Venezuela as a "significant obstacle" have grown over time from 77% of respondents in 2012 to 93% in 2016, reflecting that the issue has grown acute. Furthermore, according to the World Bank, Venezuela also scores significantly lower than average on controls of corruption and regulatory quality—scores that have fallen significantly over the past decade.

Over the years, new types of corruption risks have emerged as Venezuela has fallen into political and economic chaos. In particular, the current environment in Venezuela makes it difficult for local companies to perform basic compliance tasks, and for parent companies to exercise proper compliance oversight of their local subsidiaries. In this way, FCPA risks tend to arise in tangible and intangible ways.

Widespread state ownership. The more ownership that the state has in the local economy, the more opportunity for FCPA problems to arise. Over the years in Venezuela, the government has begun to participate in sectors as diverse as energy, food, clothing, telecommunications, and automobiles, either through joint ventures or expropriation. Such state involvement greatly increases the potential touch points that companies can have with "foreign officials."

For example, companies doing business with PDVSA, the state-owned oil company that was a source of bribe requests in the FCPA action against Pride International, commonly experience a variety of corruption risks. In the Pride case, PDSVA cancelled or unexpectedly failed to renew leases for the company's offshore drilling rigs, and then contacted the company asking for monthly payments to the board to continue the contracts. PDSVA also failed to pay Pride for services performed until the company engaged a third party who bribed a PDSVA executive. Oil and gas projects are often held up due to lack of funds, creating leverage for PDVSA officials to demand improper payments from companies to keep engagements going. PDVSA frequently falls behind on paying its bills to service providers, which has generated a cottage industry of third-party collection agencies that can be attractive, and risky, to companies owed thousands, if not millions, of dollars.

Currency controls. Venezuela's currency exchange controls, designed to stem capital flight and inflation, create both accounting and bribery risks for companies. Companies often look for creative ways to remove their money from the country. A thriving black market offers up to ten times the primary exchange rate offered by the government. Agents regularly pitch their services for moving currency through offshore channels. Local service providers often request that fees be paid outside of the country. Because these practices are pervasive, they have even great potential to create FCPA accounting violations. Moreover, under local currency regimes, if a company (or its agent) can convince the government that its imports are vital to the local economy, it can obtain a more preferential official exchange rate for their purchase, which also raises bribery risks.

The law of fair prices. The enactment in 2014 of the Law of Fair Prices (the *Ley Orgánica de Precios Justos*) has made it difficult for some companies to stay profitable, because cost structures are subject to central control. At the same time, if the company reduces or shuts down its operations, it can risk violating the same law, which prohibits "boycott" and "sabotage" of the local economy. Companies that reduce normal operations can be subject to penalties like suspension of business, confiscation of goods, and revocation of business licenses. In addition, company personnel can be subject to criminal fines, as well as jail time. As a result, many companies feel a squeeze from two different directions. Employees, too, might be tempted to bribe an official who threatens to shut down a company's operations, based on a fear of going to jail. Company personnel might also make improper payments to reduce costs and keep their company afloat, such as to reduce customs duties or to obtain regulatory approvals to downsize workforces.

Security and intimidation concerns. Violence in Venezuela is high. A homicide rate of approximately 5,000 in 1998 has grown to an estimated 25,000 in 2013. When a company's workforce has legitimate concerns of their own personal safety, it is difficult to persuade them to pay particular attention to corruption risks. Moreover, people are generally afraid of doing something that could upset the government. Intimidation by security forces means that employees might not be comfortable discussing corruption risks at group compliance trainings. Due diligence on third parties is complicated when people are wary of sharing detailed information about other companies. FCPA internal investigations are frustrated when interviewees refuse to talk about government officials, fearing that meeting rooms might be bugged or that conversations will be shared.

The brain drain. Because so many talented compliance professionals have left the country, international companies are finding it difficult to identify qualified local personnel to manage their anti-corruption compliance programs on the ground. Not only is local capacity in corporate compliance, financial controls, and other key areas becoming scarce, but also companies find it difficult simply to recruit local professionals who speak English and are, thus, positioned to communicate more easily with head offices in the United States, Europe, and elsewhere. Where talent does exist, companies are competitively fighting over it.

Chapter 4

Conveying Anti-Corruption Compliance to Latin American Business Leaders

In some countries, corporate anti-corruption compliance can challenge fundamental legal concepts and deeply held assumptions about how enforcement should work. Latin America is no exception. The idea that companies can be held criminally liable for the corrupt acts of their employees is not an accepted legal principle in many Latin American jurisdictions. Holding companies liable for the corrupt acts of their third-party providers, especially if they have no knowledge of those corrupt acts, might seem even more outlandish. But perhaps the most preposterous idea is conducting an internal investigation of one's own company when allegations of wrongdoing arise, and disclosing the findings to government authorities. As a result, conveying these anti-corruption principals accurately and in a way that resonates with Latin American employees requires time and care.

Nevertheless, local companies are increasingly seeking guidance on how – as compliance expert Tom Fox says – to "do compliance." In the 2016 Latin America Corruption Survey, 78% of respondents working for local or regional companies said that management of their companies has taken steps to protect their companies from corruption risk, compared to 94% of respondents from multinational companies. Still, only 45% of respondents who work for local and regional companies said that dealing with corruption is a "top priority," compared to 69% at multinational companies.

Below are some proven "best practices" when educating corporate leaders in Latin America about compliance.

Setting the Stage

In Latin America, informal conversations are one of the most effective ways to communicate with executives about anti-corruption compliance. Formal presentations in boardrooms, executive suites, and at management conferences can be helpful, but FCPA practitioners tend to make the most headway moving anti-corruption up a manager's priority list during less-charged conversations at cocktail parties, in airport lounges, or at the occasional birthday gathering. This approach makes sense. Addressing highly sensitive issues like corruption in formal settings can feel risky and off-putting. Who wants to publicly acknowledge that one of their peers might be paying bribes? In Latin America, casual settings are more conducive to sensitive, one-on-one conversations.

When engaging Latin American leaders one-on-one in informal settings, it is helpful to emphasize the following four points to drive home the importance of compliance.

Compliance is a basic business standard. For companies doing international business, anti-corruption compliance is no longer an option; it is a basic requirement. In today's global marketplace, executives should anticipate frequent questions about their company's anti-corruption compliance efforts from various stakeholders, including joint venture partners, customers, shareholders, external auditors, enforcement officials, lenders, and purchasers, just to name a few. The more that a company can demonstrate responsible business practices, the more favorable it will be in the eyes of a foreign investor or partner, giving it a competitive advantage.

FCPA penalties can be massive. The most expensive FCPA settlements involving bribes in Latin America include: Siemens (US$800 million in penalties in 2008), Alcatel-Lucent S.A. (US$137 million in penalties in 2010), Hewlett Packard (US$108 million in penalties in 2015), ABB Ltd. (US$58.3 million in penalties in 2010), and Pride International (US$56 million in penalties in 2010). In addition to fines and penalties, many enforcement actions also involve the appointment of monitors, jail time for executives, shareholder derivative lawsuits, and damaged reputations. Anti-corruption compliance programs can go a long way toward reducing sanctions and avoiding other negative consequences.

Legal costs can be just as significant. The costs related to a government investigation are considerable. In May 2015, Wal-Mart announced that it had spent over US$600 million on costs related to conducting an internal investigation and improving its compliance program. Similarly, Petrobras' chief executive officer said in a conference call in 2015 that the company's internal investigation into alleged corruption is expected to cost US$57 million for that year alone. Even the most expensive FCPA settlement of all time—Siemens's US$800 million payment to the SEC and the DOJ—was less than the reported US$1 billion the company spent on its internal investigation. Companies can greatly reduce the cost of a government investigation by already having a compliance program in place.

Anti-corruption laws abound. The United States is no longer the only relevant anti-corruption enforcement authority in the Americas. Countries like Brazil, Chile, Colombia, Mexico, and Peru also have made significant enhancements to local laws over the last few years, many of which have been pursuant to joining the OECD Anti-Bribery Convention. In addition to new laws, some Latin American countries are showing a greater interest in establishing serious enforcement regimes. Given this, compliance officers should remind employees in Latin America not to lose sight of other non-FCPA laws. This also includes the UKBA. The UKBA's Corporate Offense has jurisdictional elements that are arguably even broader than the FCPA, extending to the corrupt acts of companies with ongoing operations in the U.K., even if those acts have nothing to do with the United Kingdom. Since many of these legal frameworks offer companies credit for anti-corruption compliance programs, investing in compliance allows companies to stay ahead of the curve.

Describing the FCPA's Anti-Bribery Provisions

The FCPA's anti-bribery provisions make it illegal for foreign persons acting in the United States, or U.S. companies or individuals acting anywhere in the world, to give or promise to give anything of value to a foreign official, directly or indirectly, to obtain or retain business or gain an unfair advantage.

Government contracting, in particular, is an extremely high area of risk. The OECD's 2014 Foreign Bribery Report, for example, concluded that 57% of the 427 transnational bribery cases investigated, prosecuted, and concluded by members of the OECD Anti-Bribery Convention between 1999 and 2014 involved bribes that were promised, offered, or given to obtain contracts through public procurement.

Gift, travel, and entertainment expenses are another area where potential bribery risks lurk. This is supported by FCPA enforcement actions involving Latin America under the statute's anti-bribery provisions. For example, in 2005, the oil services software company Paradigm treated an official at the Mexican state-owned oil company Pemex to a US$12,000 birthday trip to Napa Valley, California, and also spent another US$10,000 entertaining the same official in Mexico. This and other conduct ran afoul of the FCPA's anti-bribery provisions, forcing the company to sign a non-prosecution agreement in 2007.

Bribery risks exist in many other business areas, as well. Consider, for example, the former executives of American Rice, David Kay and Douglas Murphy, who were found guilty in 2005 of bribing Haitian officials to reduce their company's taxes. Others, like the ongoing Wal-Mart investigation involving Mexico, relate to bribery payments made to obtain permits, licenses, and registrations. The Siemens Argentina case involved improper payments to influence lawsuits. FCPA actions in other regions have involved donations to charities headed by government officials in return for business benefits.

Once company leaders understand the broad array of activities that can constitute bribery, anti-corruption compliance begins to take on more importance.

Emphasizing the FCPA's Accounting Provisions

It is important to emphasize to Latin American executives that, under the FCPA, companies can be punished not only for their own wrongful acts, like paying bribes, but also for acts that they do not commit. In particular, the FCPA's accounting provisions require companies to have internal controls in place. Companies that do not have certain protections like appropriate accounting systems and anti-corruption policies, procedures, and processes, risk violating the law for not doing what is otherwise required.

Because of this, Latin American executives should be careful not to focus exclusively on the FCPA's bribery prohibitions and ignore its accounting provisions. For companies listed in the United States, the accounting provisions are equally, if not more, important. They follow something close to a strict liability standard, not requiring authorities to establish corrupt intent.

Specifically, the FCPA's accounting provisions require U.S. and foreign companies registered on any U.S. securities exchange to make and keep books and records in reasonable detail to accurately and fairly reflect transactions and disbursements of the company's assets and to devise and maintain a system of internal accounting controls that ensures transactions are executed in accordance with management's authorization.

As more Latin American companies go public in the United States, the relevance of these rules in the region will only grow. Even if a Latin American company is not listed in the United States, it still might have to follow accounting requirements if it is a subsidiary or partner of a U.S.-listed company. Since a publicly traded company's books and records include those of its consolidated subsidiaries and affiliates, that company's responsibility extends to ensuring that subsidiaries, joint ventures, and other partnerships under its control also comply with the accounting provisions.

Books and records violations. Companies operating in Latin America have committed, or have been accused of committing, various types of books and records violations under the FCPA's accounting provisions.

The medical device company Biomet's violations in Brazil and Argentina, for example, involved mischaracterizations of bribes in the company's books, such as falsely recording bribes to Brazilian doctors as "commissions." In general, accounting violations occur when bribes are concealed as legitimate payments—such as commissions, royalties, consulting fees, sales and marketing expenses, miscellaneous expenses, or petty cash withdrawals. A violation might involve misreporting large bribe payments or widespread inaccurate recording of smaller payments made as part of a systemic pattern of bribery.

In some cases, the absence of legitimate supporting documentation to confirm a payment's actual recipient and purpose will constitute the FCPA violation. For example, the health product company Nature's Sunshine made undocumented cash payments to Brazilian customs brokers, some of which were passed along to customs officials, to gain entry of unregistered products into Brazil. The company booked the cash payments as "importation advances," but it failed to maintain any receipts or other documents supporting this characterization. In general, when employees use cash to make business payments, maintaining supporting documentation is particularly important.

Similarly, FCPA violations can occur when companies obtain false documentation to make it appear that payments are legitimate. Thus, in the Nature's Sunshine case, after making cash payments to Brazilian customs agents without supporting documentation, the company began purchasing fictitious supporting documentation to attempt to conceal the actual purpose of the payments. In another example, in the Biomet case, employees of the company's Argentine subsidiary obtained phony invoices from doctors stating that payments to them were for professional services or consulting when, in fact, no legitimate services were provided. Instead, employees made the payments in exchange for sales of the company's medical devices. In the Siemens case involving Venezuela, the company created sham equipment supply contracts to justify illicit payments made through a consultant.

Internal controls violations. The types of controls that companies are expected to have in place as part of their internal controls framework are diverse. Some might be described as "accounting" in nature, and others are additional processes that companies are expected to apply to high-risk business activities.

At the most basic level, accounting controls must ensure that company funds are not used for bribery. This means that (1) individuals with approval power for expenses are independent and have properly delegated authority; (2) approvals are based on supporting documentation; (3) transactions are properly and accurately recorded; (4) processes are regularly monitored, audited, and tested; and, (5) finance personnel is trained to spot corruption red flags.

Common accounting controls include the following:

➢ **Accounts Payable.** Controls should be designed to ensure that types and amounts of the items and services invoiced to the company are legitimate and correctly correspond to the values and descriptions in written contracts, as well as the supporting documentation. Payments should be authorized against original invoices, and invoice numbers should be checked against files to prevent duplicate invoicing. Companies can require special approvals for payments to account numbers not on the master file, manual payments, and unusual or unfamiliar vendors. The monitoring and testing program should give particular attention to variations in the normal purchasing process, unusual vendors, split payments to avoid authorized payment thresholds amounts, duplicate payments, and frequent payments to the same vendor. When these controls are not in place, companies are susceptible to books and records violations as well, as discussed above.

➤ **Expense Reimbursement.** Written travel and hospitality policies should establish standard expense reimbursement rules. They can require approvals from management, the submission of original backup documentation, and the timely entry of expense reports. Companies should keep records of the identities of recipients of funds, the business purposes of the expenses, and internal authorizations required and received. Heightened oversight should be applied to expenses made on behalf of non-employees, which can include pre-approvals and special value and frequency limits.

➤ **Payroll.** Payroll responsibilities should be segregated for activities like data entry of employee details, authorizations, and payments. Any changes to payroll files, such as salary increases, should include supporting documentation and be approved by someone other than the person inputting the information. Department heads should regularly review and approve payment reports to ensure that salary recipients currently work for the company.

➢ **Petty Cash.** Companies should adopt written policies governing the disbursement of petty cash that dictate appropriate and authorized uses. Policies should ensure that access to petty cash is limited and subject to approvals, and that reimbursements are based on supporting documentation and sufficient detail about use. Companies should frequently conduct reconciliations of petty cash disbursements.

➢ **Claims.** Written policies for management of claims, such as returned goods or disputed services, should establish consistent methods for handling these issues. This can include requiring claims to be supported by documentation, recorded properly, and approved by someone not involved in the original transaction.

➢ **Internal Audit.** A capable internal audit function should be in place to identify wrongdoing or act on red flags. In the Biomet case, when internal audit identified that royalties were paid to surgeons purchasing the company's medical devices, it sought only to confirm that the amounts paid were recorded in the books. It took no steps to determine *why* the royalties were paid to doctors. Nor did it seek evidence of the services provided in return for the payments. Instead, the internal audit report concluded that there were adequate controls in place to properly account for the royalties paid.

Certain non-accounting processes might not constitute traditional notions of "internal controls," but Latin American executives should know that FCPA enforcement officials have taken the position that a wide range of activities is covered under this term.

Such activities include:

➤ **Anti-corruption compliance program.** Companies are expected to design and implement an adequate anti-corruption compliance program, which includes policies and procedures that minimize risks that bribes will be paid. BellSouth was subject to an FCPA enforcement action for its practices in Nicaragua and Venezuela when it lacked basic compliance functions for its business there.

➤ **Vendor relationships.** Companies reduce the risk that their third parties will pay bribes on their behalf by placing controls over the selection and performance of vendors. A vendor selection process should require that multiple providers are considered and compared, selection is based on quality and price, and decisions are made according to delegations of authority. Companies should conduct risk-based third party due diligence and monitoring. In addition, vendor selection and use should be periodically and randomly audited to ensure processes are followed and no red flags are present. In the Eli Lilly enforcement action, the SEC found that the company lacked sufficient controls when it failed to have a due diligence and monitoring process in place to ensure its Brazilian distributors were not paying bribes on its behalf. In the Siemens action involving Argentina, the company used consultants as conduits for bribes.

➤ **Gift-giving.** Companies should implement specific policies to ensure that gifts are given for legitimate purposes, such as to promote general goodwill, visibility, or reputation, and not to improperly influence an official to secure an improper advantage. Specific policies should prohibit cash gifts, establish pre-authorized value and frequency limits, create special authorization requirements for higher valued gifts, track aggregate amounts, consider local laws, and ensure supporting documentation with the names of recipients and business purposes.

> **Charitable donations and political contributions.** Controls should ensure that a company's charitable donations and political donations are not, in fact, disguised bribes. Policies should require such disbursements to be reviewed by senior compliance officials. Processes should confirm that recipients are legitimate and do not create integrity concerns, principals and officers of charitable organizations are not linked to public officials, and recipients of political contributions are not positioned to improperly benefit the company.

> **Human resources.** A company's HR Department has an important role to play in its anti-corruption program. For example, it can conduct background checks on new employees for integrity-related issues, identify when employees are related to public officials, and ensure that new employees receive anti-corruption compliance training. HR can help administer both incentive and disciplinary measures related to employee compliance. It can also probe compliance issues during exit interviews. In the Tyson Foods case in Mexico, the company's payroll system was manipulated to transfer bribes to the wives of health inspection officials.

> **Training.** Companies should effectively communicate their anti-corruption policies and procedures to their employees and, where necessary, their third parties consultants and agents. Training programs should convey appropriate compliance lessons to targeted audiences, providing examples

of practical cases and common red flags. For example, in the Orthofix case, the SEC found that the company failed to maintain adequate internal controls when the company's FCPA-related training, and compliance policy, in Mexico were provided only in English and not in Spanish. Trainings should be documented and repeated periodically.

The notion that the mere existence of "controls" can take on a level of importance that is equal to prohibiting bribery itself is new to many business leaders in Latin America. Under the FCPA, establishing a controls regime can be key for prohibiting bribery, complying with the FCPA's accounting provisions, and establishing a culture of compliance.

Highlighting the Riskiness of Bribery

In the SEC's FCPA action against employees of Direct Access Partners in connection with a bribery scheme in Venezuela, the SEC proclaimed that there is "no honor among thieves," highlighting the inherent riskiness of bribe-tainted transactions. One of the facts alleged in that case was that the U.S. participants falsified the amounts of their fraudulent fees in their reports to a Venezuelan official, thereby deceiving the person to whom they were paying kickbacks. The U.S. traders were taking more than they promised. In the Siemens action involving Argentina, it was the foreign officials who engaged in the deception. Despite paying millions to Argentine authorities, Siemens Argentina never received the US$1 billion contract to supply identification cards to the country's citizens that it was promised. Political leadership in Argentina shifted and new demands for illicit payments were made. Each leader wanted his or her piece of the action.

Engaging in bribery creates various, possibly unintended, dynamics and results. This reality, when explained to Latin American executives, can help convey the importance of anti-corruption compliance.

Risky elements of bribery include:

Warped motivations. In bribery schemes, the absence of ethics is well established. Bribery always involves people motivated by money and greed and willing to break the rules. Participants in schemes might choose to deceive one another. In Latin America, "putting one over" on the United States business person involved might even be a source of pride. Corrupt officials might never have the intention of following through with a scheme in the first place.

Lack of enforceability. Unenforceability of corruption schemes is another fundamental problem of bribery. Schemes are usually not based on written contracts, and participants cannot take non-compliance to court. The other option might be to seek assistance from criminal networks. But this implicates another set of problems. As a result, the deceived are often left standing with empty hands.

Unexpected complexity. Once a person engages in a bribery scheme, it is hard to stop or extricate himself or herself from it. This might not matter if a scheme is simple and straightforward, but schemes usually are not. They usually involve numerous actors, like agents and consultants, accountants, and anyone else recruited to help cover up tracks. As such, schemes can grow complex in unexpected ways. As demonstrated in the Siemens Argentina case, when personnel changes, parties need to renegotiate terms and conclude new deals. The foreign official might not be the only one that changes. New auditors might enter the fold. Consultants might switch. No matter how hard one tries, corrupt arrangements have a way of getting out of control.

Keeping everyone happy. When several participants are involved, they must all be kept happy. Each is involved in the secret, and each has the ability to blow up the plan. The task of maintaining buy-in is made more complicated by the fact that, these days, each participant has the ability to exercise the SEC whistleblower mechanisms, even if he or she is implicated. Under the U.S. Dodd-Frank Act, even guilty whistleblowers can recover bounties, and have done so.

Explaining Declinations and the Meaning of "Rogue Employee"

When companies have strong compliance programs in place, they stand to receive cooperation credit in the event that an FCPA violation occurs. FCPA enforcement officials might also decide not to bring a case against the company, known as a "declination."

Instead, the U.S. government might proceed against only the responsible individuals.

This is what occurred in the Morgan Stanley case. After investigating the firm's dealings in China, the DOJ and the SEC decided not to pursue an FCPA action against the firm. Instead, they pursued action against Garth Peterson, the firm's former managing director for real estate in China. U.S. enforcement officials claimed that Peterson oversaw a secret scheme to pay almost US$2 million to himself and a Chinese official, and to help the official acquire valuable land in Shanghai. Peterson wound up facing imprisonment for conspiring to evade internal accounting controls that the FCPA required Morgan Stanley to keep. In addition to serving jail time, Peterson agreed to pay US$250,000 in disgorgement and forfeit US$3.4 million in Chinese real estate.

Morgan Stanley was not held liable for any misconduct, despite the existence of FCPA-related violations, because of its robust compliance program. In fact, the Chief of the SEC's FCPA unit said that Morgan Stanley went "out of its way" to ensure that its policies were being followed.

According to the DOJ, Morgan Stanley took the following steps that influenced the government's decision not to bring an enforcement action:

➢ Maintained a system of internal controls meant to ensure accountability for its assets and to prevent employees from offering, promising or paying anything of value to foreign government officials.

➤ Had internal policies that were updated regularly to reflect regulatory developments and specific risks, prohibited bribery, and addressed corruption risks associated with the giving of gifts, business entertainment, travel, lodging, meals, charitable contributions and employment.

➤ Frequently trained its employees on its internal policies, the FCPA and other anti-corruption laws. Between 2002 and 2008, Morgan Stanley trained various groups of Asia-based personnel on anti-corruption policies 54 times. During the same period, Morgan Stanley trained Peterson on the FCPA seven times and reminded him to comply with the FCPA at least 35 times.

➤ Regularly monitored transactions, randomly audited particular employees, transactions and business units, and tested to identify illicit payments.

➤ Conducted extensive due diligence on all new business partners and imposed stringent controls on payments made to business partners.

Morgan Stanley is not the only company to receive a declination in an FCPA case. In fact, declinations can be common. The DOJ and the SEC give examples of other declinations in *A Resource Guide to the U.S. Foreign Corrupt Practices Act* ("FCPA Resource Guide").

As was shown in the Morgan Stanley case, enforcement officials continually emphasize that employees are only "rogue" if compliance programs are otherwise adequate. If a company claims to have a rogue employee, and an investigation then reveals violations in five other countries, that claim will seem less credible. If the company cannot show internal controls at the time of the violation or a program has failed to catch a decades-long corruption scheme, enforcement officials will be more likely to find the company legally responsible. Stressing these aspects of corporate liability when teaching Latin American executives about the FCPA can put corporate compliance in a more valuable light.

Demonstrating How FCPA Compliance Is Good For The Bottom Line

In many Latin American business circles, the terms "compliance" and "revenue generation" are considered contradictory. "Compliance" is a cost center. It also keeps companies from engaging in transactions that would otherwise make money.

Latin American business leaders can be shown that, in fact, robust anti-corruption compliance programs bring with them business benefits, which can be critical in increasingly competitive global markets. The following considerations help highlight the point.

Compliance projects strength. When a company sends a consistent message that it conducts itself ethically, foreign officials are less likely to ask for bribes. Conversely, tolerating improper payments is a slippery slope. Once foreign officials identify a company as one that will pay bribes, the requests become more frequent and the amounts much larger. Sergio Cicero Zapata, the former Wal-Mart de Mexico executive who reportedly ran its bribery scheme, told the

New York Times about "contending with 'greedy' officials who jacked up bribe demands."

Tolerating bribery leads to business uncertainty. Off-the-books accounts set up to pay bribes can be used for other fraud and other abuses. When executives use hidden accounts to withdraw money to pay bribes, they are also able to embezzle money from those accounts for their own purposes. Once a certain level of illegality is tolerated in an organization, problems can grow dramatically. In contrast, adhering to the rule of law helps ensure certainty and continuity.

Compliance improves quality control. Compliance procedures create a protective check on the types of partners with whom a company chooses to do business. Due diligence and monitoring help identify which third parties are essential, and weed out the ones that are not. M&A due diligence for corruption issues means that acquired businesses are fully vetted. When employees are not focused on hiding schemes, they can focus their efforts instead on improving the quality of their goods and services.

Compliance serves as a long-term investment in reputation. The cost of an enforcement action is not only the fine, it is also the consequences of a damaged reputation in the marketplace. No company wants to be known as the poster child for a new and unique bribery scheme revealed in an FCPA matter.

When well-designed internal controls are in place, companies are positioned to operate more efficiently. Robust internal controls create accountability that leads better performance. They also help companies obtain better information about their businesses—the types of sales practices being used, the circumstances that employees confront in the field, and the obstacles that logistics teams experience. When companies better understand the landscape, they can structure operations to respond more effectively and are positioned to more deftly navigate pitfalls.

Employees tend to have better morale when they work for companies committed to doing business the right way. Better morale leads to better productivity. On the other hand, working for an organization that tolerates unlawful activity, or that has lax and inconsistently applied rules, can frustrate the focus on the work itself.

A good case example for this concept is that of Siemens, a company that bolstered its compliance program with the quality of German engineering after its blockbuster corruption fine. Siemens's compliance personnel now like to discuss how the company's two most profitable years occurred after its FCPA enforcement action and subsequent compliance improvements. The company's business flourished, even in a tightly controlled environment. They state that the enforcement action shook the company, and the compliance program helped rebuild morale. Business partners once again saw Siemens as a trustworthy company. The costs of its products no longer reflected hidden costs. One could say that Siemens is a poster child for the proposition that, when compliance is done right, it is good for business.

Chapter 5

Tailored Compliance Strategies for Companies in Latin America

One key message that FCPA enforcement officials convey over and over again is that off-the-shelf, check-the-box compliance programs provide little value to a company. They are not sufficient to compel effective compliance within an organization. In the event of an enforcement action, such lax measures will not generate meaningful credit for the company in the eyes of FCPA enforcement officials. Instead, programs should be dynamic, interactive, and responsive to actual and specific risks that employees encounter in the course of their day-to-day roles and responsibilities. To do this effectively in Latin America, companies can follow specific compliance strategies that have seemed to work particularly well. To be sure, companies apply the following approaches in their operations no matter the region of the world. But in Latin America, these approaches tend to be particularly effective in helping companies implement programs on the ground.

The Importance of Risk-Based Programs in Latin America

Companies doing business in Latin America do not have unlimited compliance budgets. Complicating matters, the diversity of risks in the region mean that companies can become lost or overwhelmed trying to manage every risk, big and small, that their personnel face.

How do companies address this challenge? They tailor their compliance strategies to actual risks. Whether one follows the guidance of the U.S. Federal Sentencing Guidelines, heeds the advice of the FCPA Resource Guide, listens to statements from enforcers themselves, or analyzes FCPA enforcement actions, it is clear that enforcement officials expect compliance efforts to be risk based. Understanding this basic concept will help companies bridge the gap between seemingly impossible compliance expectations and creating an acceptable program that works in practice. As James Tillen, vice chair of Miller & Chevalier's International Department commonly says, "Compliance begins with the premise that every company's anti-corruption compliance program must be tailored to its particular risk profile and resources, and that one size does not fit all."

In Latin America, tailoring compliance strategies to risk means focusing compliance efforts on the highest risk countries, industries, and transactions. Transparency International's 2015 CPI ranks Venezuela and Haiti as the countries perceived as being the most corrupt in the region, followed by Nicaragua, Paraguay, Guatemala,

Honduras, Argentina, Ecuador, the Dominican Republic, Bolivia, and Mexico. All of these are ranked in the top 50% of the most high-risk countries in the world. Many other key Latin American markets, like Colombia, Brazil, and Peru, are not far behind. If companies are doing business in these countries, they should be targeting their compliance dollars accordingly.

In addition, some industries also are considered higher risk than others and deserve more compliance attention. This point was highlighted in remarks given in 2014 by then senior deputy of the Fraud Section of the DOJ Criminal Division, James Koukios. In his remarks, Koukios offered some rare insight to lawyers and compliance specialists throughout Latin America. He described the industries that pose the highest risk in the region, based on the DOJ's own evidence from past and ongoing corruption investigations. Specifically, Koukios highlighted the extractive, utilities, and health sectors in Latin America as particularly risk-prone, because they are often under government control or ownership or involve the provision of public goods. Companies that work in the oil and gas sector in the region, for example, confront regular business with state-owned oil companies as diverse as Petrobras, Pemex, Ecopetrol, YPF, PDVSA, PetroPeru, PetroEcuador, PetroMinerales, Hocol, CENIT, and Petrotrin. Enforcement officials expect any company that is engaged in a high-risk sector to have its guard up.

The U.S. government's expectation of risk-based programs puts a premium on formal risk assessments. FCPA enforcement officials expect companies to think critically about how they engage third parties in high risk jurisdictions, where they engage in public contracting, and where they have relationships with foreign officials. The DOJ's former chief FCPA enforcer, Patrick Stokes, once explained that the DOJ does not go into a meeting with a company expecting to see specific compliance measures. Instead, the DOJ wants companies to identify for themselves their highest risks and explain how they are addressing those risks: "Just as we don't want companies to have a check-the-box program, we don't have one for evaluating them."

Kara Brockmeyer, Chief of the FCPA Unit of the SEC's Enforcement Division, said at a conference in 2014 that to understand FCPA risk, compliance personnel have to "get out into the field." They need to speak with their workforces about how they do business, understand where they have government touch points, and ensure that controls are structured appropriately to prevent improper payments in high-risk areas. Companies also need to keep their risk assessments up-to-date. Business activities change, and companies need to understand corruption risk implications when they do. A company might have a Mexico-based manufacturing facility that only sells to the United States. When it purchases another facility in the country with significant sales to the Mexican government, its FCPA risk profile changes. When it further acquires a company in Central America as part of a regional expansion, additional compliance steps are necessary.

Risk-based compliance also means that compliance programs will never be fool-proof. Issues could arise in lower risk areas of the company's business. Enforcers understand this. As Stokes once said, "We have no expectation that a compliance program will be perfect and is going to catch all bad conduct. We understand that bad actors will try to work around controls and try to evade them. But we expect that programs are well thought out to prevent this." Despite failing to stop an improper act, if a company can show that it has taken a thoughtful approach to preventing compliance violations, and that it has focused on highest areas of risk, then it has positioned itself to put forth a reasonable defense.

In comments at a Trace International conference in Mexico in 2013, Alexandra Wrage put her own spin on the concept of reasonable compliance and a company's responsibility for the actions of rogue employees: "The government understands that, when you pick an employee, you are not hiring them to take care of your children. You are hiring them to advance your interests in legal and appropriate ways. The government also knows you might make mistakes. What they want is for you to take a reasonable and consistent approach [to compliance measures]." The important part of this advice is that a company should be able to tell a credible story of concrete steps it has taken to address actual risk.

The FCPA Resource Guide reaffirms the importance of risk-based compliance. For example, when companies rely on numerous third-party relationships, the guidance advises that a risk-based approach to due diligence is essential: "DOJ and SEC will give meaningful credit to a company that implements in good faith a comprehensive, risk-based compliance program, even if that program does not prevent an infraction in a low risk area because greater attention and resources had been devoted to a higher risk area."

Targeting Compliance Training to Latin American Employees

In the 2016 Latin America Corruption Survey, 85% of respondents who worked at multinational companies said that their companies conduct compliance training, while less than half of respondents who worked at local and regional companies said that their companies do so. Wherever it is conducted, FCPA compliance training should cover some basics areas—such as anti-corruption enforcement trends, elements of bribery and books and records/internal controls offenses, common forms of FCPA-prohibited activity, the consequences of non-compliance, industries and sectors under the enforcement microscope, and the specifics of the company's own compliance program.

Below are some additional training best practices that can be particularly helpful in Latin America for encouraging employees' adherence to compliance:

Use local language. Many participants in the region do not speak English. Even if they do, compliance concepts are communicated more effectively if trainings are conducted in the local languages of the region, or else certain key issues could be lost in translation. Employees also might not feel comfortable asking questions in a language other than their native one.

Discuss specific and relevant cases. Trainers should tell sensational bribery stories from prior enforcement actions, preferably ones involving their industries and countries, to capture employees' attention. For example, even though the U.S. enforcement action against FIFA executives and related parties from Argentina and Brazil does not involve the FCPA, it does involve corruption and soccer and can be a helpful case study in a region where passion for soccer is second to none.

In Argentina, trainers can discuss the Ball Corporation case, in which the company's CEO used the sale of his personal luxury car to pay kickbacks. In Brazil, trainers can share snippets of e-mail between a Dallas Airmotive manager and a Brazilian Air Force sergeant that appear in the company's deferred prosecution agreement. In particular, the company manager e-mails the sergeant: "Tell me, my friend, is everything alright there?? And the hotel is so-so or worth the expense??? I hope that you are enjoying it," to which the sergeant replied: "When I said I had confidence in your good taste, I confess that I underestimated you... hehe The Hotel was excellent. I believe that it was a great present to [my wife]. She insists on passing on thanks to you. Great job, my good friend!!!" In Costa Rica, trainers can cite the example of how Alcatel hired a consultant – that was a perfume company – to provide telecommunications advice, which made the business justification of the engagement problematic when U.S. authorities reviewed it. Finally, in Mexico, trainers can include details of what sound like scenes from a movie: BizJet agents literally carrying bags of cash across the U.S.-Mexico border to bribe officials.

Make trainings interactive. Following a dry PowerPoint that discusses only black-letter law can put employees to sleep, especially in Latin America where audiences value engagement and interaction. Latin Americans like to take part in role plays, participate in discussions on risk, and ask unfiltered questions. When this happens, employees are more likely to absorb and remember compliance concepts. The scenarios used to convey concepts should be ones that are most relevant in the Latin American context. For example, using a description of a golf outing with a foreign official as an example of high-risk entertainment might not have the strongest impact in Brazil, where golf is not as popular a sport as it is in other parts of the world. Instead, an example of an outing relating to the America's Cup sailing competition might have more impact as an example.

Explain how violations are discovered. When learning about the FCPA, Latin Americans often assume that the chances of enforcement officials discovering bribery are minimal, especially given how rare it is that local anti-corruption laws are enforced. Trainers should make clear that issues can be brought to the attention of U.S. authorities in numerous ways—such as through media reports, whistleblower complaints, industry competitors, or the Federal Bureau of Investigation ("the FBI"). Employees may be interested to hear about increasingly aggressive investigative tactics being deployed today by FCPA investigators, including body wires worn by cooperating witnesses in cases like Petrotiger in Colombia and BizJet in Mexico to obtain evidence against executives, who were later charged with FCPA-related violations.

Describe how individuals can be liable. During anti-corruption training, employees tend to pay more attention when they realize that *they* can be individually liable for FCPA violations, since this usually translates into prison time. Such warnings apply equally to employees outside the United States and to U.S. citizens. Indeed, U.S.

enforcement officials have not shied away from spreading the juris-dictional net widely to the Latin American region. Take, for example, the Venezuelan bribe receiver in the Direct Access Partners case, who was arrested for FCPA-related issues while traveling to Miami. In another example, a former manager at French telecommunications company Alcatel, who was responsible for bribe payments in Costa Rica, was arrested by U.S. authorities while traveling through Miami and eventually pled guilty in the U.S. courts. In 2015, Deputy Attorney General Sally Yates issued a memorandum instructing U.S. prosecutors to prioritize individual liability in all of their investigations, which can implicate non-U.S. citizens as well.

Show how various company actors have a role to play in compliance. A company's chief compliance officer is not the only one in the organization responsible for compliance. Individuals throughout the company have important roles to play. The CEO must establish tone from the top. The internal auditor must build FCPA compliance testing into reviews. Business unit leaders must know how to spot red flags. The more employees understand these multiple responsibilities, the more they begin to appreciate them. In Latin America, this sometimes requires heightened attention, because traditional corporate roles might differ from the way they are commonly understood in the United States. For example, while the general counsel in many U.S. companies is a core member of the company's top management team participating in both business and legal decisions, in Latin America the position is often relegated to a legal service support function. This might be adequate for fulfilling legal duties, but it is not always adequate for fulfilling compliance duties. To make a compliance program work effectively, the general counsel will often need to offer advice on business matters, since business decisions can implicate a wide range of risks, including compliance with the FCPA.

Remind employees that corruption also exists in the United States. Because some Latin American employees might take issue with the fact that the FCPA targets the corrupt acts of only officials outside the United States, it is helpful to address this issue at the outset of training. The trainer can explain, for example, that other laws in the United States address domestic corruption. The trainer can show pictures of U.S. officials being carried away in handcuffs for committing domestic bribery. Steps like these help ensure that Latin American employees do not feel that they are being unfairly targeted by U.S. enforcement officials.

Inform employees that the FCPA is not the only anti-corruption law being enforced around the world. It is helpful to discuss the web of international anti-corruption laws, treaties, and enforcement agencies currently in place, including local anti-bribery laws in the Latin American countries where the company operates. For example, Brazilian prosecutors init ted the Petrobras corruption investigation that led to a review oı dozens of companies and individuals in various industries. In this way, trainers send the message that compliance is relevant not only to U.S. authorities, but also throughout the region and the world. Enforcement threats can come from many different directions, not just the DOJ or SEC.

Discuss the broader importance of compliance. Trainers can discuss why curbing corruption is good for their country and how corruption corrodes businesses. This lesson is particularly relevant for employees in Latin American, where high-level government officials regularly make headlines for engaging in corrupt acts. As demonstrated by recent mass protests in Brazil, Latin American employees generally are disgusted and fed up with the intermingled nature of politics, corruption, and impunity in their countries.

Properly scope the audience. In Latin America, the idea that training should extend only to "front office" employees who interact with foreign officials is a common misconception. Other employees can be pulled into corruption schemes, too, even if they have no connection to government officials. For example, some employees might manage third parties that interact with officials on the company's behalf, and they should be prepared to spot red flags. As another example, employees in finance manage the accounting controls that help a company spot corruption and ensure compliance with the FCPA's accounting provisions. Tailored FCPA training should be given to a wide range of employees within a company's organization to ensure that they know the rules, understand how their functions support FCPA compliance, and know where to report knowledge of violations. Training can be designed to give all relevant employees a role in protecting the company, no matter their level of responsibility.

Obtain meaningful endorsement of compliance principles. After trainings are over, it is important for companies to obtain formal endorsement of compliance from participants. At a basic level, a signature on a certification form is necessary and a good first step. But note that, as a general matter, the relatively casual way in which U.S. lawyers require certifications and endorsements is often inconsistent with local norms in Latin America and can cause anxiety. Latin American legal systems are generally modeled on the Portuguese or Spanish systems, which rely heavily on notaries to legalize documents. To be valid, certifications should be obtained through formal processes that employees are used to following.

Listen, respond, and follow up. Trainers should take their time and listen to questions and respond—by e-mail afterward, if necessary. They should discuss follow-up steps, including where employees can go with questions. In Latin America, in particular, giving employees the opportunity to ask questions in private with the trainer directly after a session ends can be an effective way of learning about potential compliance policy violations. Trust goes a long way. Training is just the beginning, not the end. Real endorsement begins after employees have been able to see compliance in action. Once they have participated in compliance processes, they are more likely to embrace programs more meaningfully.

Avoiding Sham Contracts and Phantom Vendors

Some of the most common bribery schemes in Latin America involve the use of sham contracts and phantom vendors. This type of scheme was highlighted in the FCPA case against Siemens in Argentina, in which the company's consulting contract with the Argentine Consulting Group involved no legitimate services and helped facilitate kickbacks to contracting officials there. A similar scheme was at the center of an FCPA enforcement action against

Ralph Lauren Corporation, in which a customs agent in Argentina billed the company for bogus services and used the funds to bribe local customs officials to clear the entry of Ralph Lauren's goods into the country. Such schemes also form the basis of many of the allegations against Petrobras and its contractors, who are accused overbilling the company and using the excess funds to give kickbacks through shell companies. An analysis conducted in 2015 by PricewaterhouseCoopers found that 22% of all FCPA cases involving Latin America between 2000 and 2015 involved the use of fictitious vendors or invoices.

The way these schemes often work in practice is that companies, or their employees, create phony written agreements with third parties, perhaps a consultant or outside vendor, or a local employee sets up a bogus consultancy or contractor. The company makes payments to the third party for purported goods or services, when in reality, the entity provides no legitimate goods or services, or not at the level to justify the compensation. The rest of the money is used for improper purposes, perhaps self-enrichment, or perhaps to bribe foreign officials to achieve some business advantage for the company.

Companies design compliance programs to address these risks by implementing controls that establish the legitimate purpose of expenditures and ensure the accurate and specific recording of the destination of funds.

In particular, the following types of controls are helpful:

Set up third-party approval systems. Pre-set processes, like vendor approval mechanisms, help reduce the possibility that a third party will be paid based on a sham contract, or that the third party is bogus. Vendor approvals require a second, and sometimes a third, set of eyes to review the agreement and assess its legitimacy before the relationship begins. One example is to require a local approval by a manager in the Latin American country and another approval by a manager at headquarters in the United States. By requiring computer databases to be populated with this information, companies further ensure that various aspects of the arrangement have been properly vetted and approved. Pre-approved vendor lists give businesses a degree of comfort that relationships are legitimate. Similarly, purchase order systems force companies to consider with whom they are dealing and what they are purchasing. It should be noted that approved vendor lists do not always avoid risks completely, since companies often allow exceptions for the use of additional vendors when they are essential and urgent. Nonetheless, such systems do create a bedrock of control. To create additional control, companies can establish budgets that anticipate expenses; pre-approval of these expenses establishes more control over dollars spent. Contracts that arise outside of the pre-approved plan can be scrutinized more closely.

Trust but verify. Companies should verify that third parties are doing what they are supposed to be doing pursuant to their contracts. Companies can do this by reviewing invoices, checks to vendors, purchase orders, inventory records, receiving documents, and other books and records for proof that goods or services were actually received. Vendors should be required to provide backup documentation to support their invoices, which should be reviewed as well.

During these reviews, companies should keep an eye out for fraudulent documentation, such as fake invoices or bogus line items. In such reviews, visuals are important. Invoices might appear unprofessional, contact information might be incomplete, invoice numbers might be in odd sequences, or numbers might be in round amounts.

To effectively identify fraudulent documentation, local knowledge of the region is essential. A non-Brazilian reviewer might not realize the odd nature of a consulting business that is based in the Planalto Paulista neighborhood in São Paulo, where very few, if any, businesses are located. And while a Google Street View search might reveal a physical building at an agent's purported address, local professionals might realize that Google is not always reliable for such searches in the local market. Rather, they will know that the company should take other steps to verify the agent's real existence. Other common red flags include payments that have no invoices, invoices that have no supporting documentation, cancelled checks with unusual endorsements, or addresses that include only P.O. Box numbers, which are generally harder to verify.

Information listed in the sales documentation should also be verified. Finance, internal audit, or compliance teams can confirm if newly purchased machinery is actually there and in use and if the broken window in the executive's office was actually replaced with a new one. If the provider is a consultant, the report issued by the consultant should be reviewed to see if it matches the description on the invoice, and discussions with the business person should take place about how the report's recommendations have been put to use.

Track, monitor, and investigate. Payments made pursuant to third-party contracts should be clearly archived in a company's books and records with specific budget codes that signify the types of goods and services at issue. Records should be made and updated in real time, while the expenses are occurring. Accurate books and records position the company to monitor contracts for potential problems.

Monitoring might include the following strategies:

➢ Compare paid vendor lists to approved vendor lists. In doing so, the company can identify which paid vendors have not yet been vetted through the normal onboarding process.

➢ Review contracts based on amounts paid to vendors, the location of the vendors, and what they are doing. For example, testing might give particular attention to contracts for periodic services, where it is sometin easier for fraud to hide. They might look closely at contracts that deal with intangibles, as opposed to physical goods, or consumable goods. Such contracts might be subject to fewer pre-existing controls, like receiving documents or inventory logs.

➢ Ask whether certain contracting personnel have shown a special interest in using a specific vendor rather than not using one at all. Reviewers might ask if all transactions with a particular vendor have been handled by only one person at the company.

➤ Look at historical patterns. Maybe a company's purchases from a particular vendor started small and then grew over time. Maybe the company frequently purchases from the vendor at a level just below that which requires additional authorization. Maybe a company started using the vendor after a particular employee joined and stopped after the employee left.

➤ Consider the possibility of phantom vendors that set up other fake vendors so that a company can receive bids from more than one source for the same work. Setting up phantom vendors makes the scheme appear more legitimate. It can also help participants inflate costs.

FCPA enforcement actions involving Latin America regularly highlight the need for accounting controls to address bogus invoicing and shell companies. In the US$22.8 million FCPA settlement with medical devices company Biomet for FCPA violations in Argentina, Brazil, and China, the failure of the company's internal audit function to fulfill compliance-related tasks was at the root of the company's FCPA issues and enabled violations to persist. The company did not review documentation supporting why commission payments were made to doctors. It did not review whether doctors performed actual and legitimate services that would have entitled them to such payments. It did not correctly classify the payments so that the books and records of the company accurately reflected the expenses. If it had performed these functions, the violations likely could have been avoided.

When designing these types of systems, verifications processes, and monitoring in Latin America, FCPA officials suggest that probing context with a critical eye is vital. In the US$29.4 million FCPA settlement with Eli Lilly concerning the activities of the company's distributor in Brazil, the SEC noted that the company's pricing committee approved the distributor's price without further inquiry. The SEC concluded that the policies and procedures Eli Lilly had in place to flag unusual discounts were deficient. It noted that the company relied on representations of the sales and marketing manager without adequate verification and analysis of the surrounding circumstances of the transactions.

In the SEC's press release, Kara Brockmeyer, the SEC's chief FCPA enforcer at the time, explained:

> Eli Lilly and its subsidiaries possessed a 'check the box' mentality when it came to third-party due diligence. Companies can't simply rely on paper-thin assurances by employees, distributors, or customers. They need to look at the surrounding circumstances of any payment to adequately assess whether it could wind up in a government official's pocket.

Such "surrounding circumstances" are often best understood by locals who know the territory.

Monitoring as a Sign of a Mature Compliance Program

If a company does not test its compliance program, the program is not effective or complete, which is a point that FCPA enforcement authorities repeatedly stress. Without a plan to monitor high-risk activities, and test compliance mechanisms in place, companies run the risk of having programs that will be seen as merely "paper" in nature. It is not enough to create a set of rules and assume that employees are following them.

At an FCPA conference in 2014, Stokes said, "Many times companies have designed a ... robust program, but [failed] to test it. What we expect is to not only have on paper a program, but to test it, to make sure it is working." DOJ will also consider whether a company has been testing its program when it considers whether to require a compliance monitor as part of an FCPA settlement. Similarly, Brockmeyer has said that, when companies go to the SEC to discuss an issue, they should expect to answer questions about how they are testing controls and where internal audit fits into the compliance program: "Bribery cannot happen if the company has control over where the money is going."

In Latin America, compliance monitoring can be particularly important because business relationships between individuals that start innocently can sometimes morph into illicit arrangements. It might take time for actors to develop a rapport that can form the basis of a corrupt plan. Jim Mintz, the founder of the investigative firm The Mintz Group, has performed investigations all over the world and remarks on how a common feature in Latin America is the deeply hidden nature of financial transactions, something that, he says, usually takes time for actors to develop. Consistent monitoring helps identify changes in relationships and red flags that might not exist at first and only arise over time. By assuming otherwise that all business relationships are as proper as when they began, companies leave themselves exposed.

Moreover, monitoring is important in Latin America because illicit plans that initially go unnoticed by compliance controls can eventually fall apart, as discussed in Chapter 4, at which point it is crucial that companies have detection systems in place. The reality that schemes do not always go as planned creates the opportunity for monitoring programs to catch instances of corruption.

How do companies test their compliance programs for indications of illicit acts? Testing can be divided into two categories: procedures testing and forensic accounting testing.

Procedures Review. Companies can test if the anti-corruption procedures currently in place are working properly. Are their head of sales, business development, and logistics fully trained on their compliance responsibilities? Are corruption risk assessments current? Are employees aware of and adhering to import and export procedures, and charitable giving rules? Are hotline tips being reviewed, categorized, and responded to in an appropriate fashion?

Companies might use their in-house compliance personnel, outside lawyers, or internal audit departments to check if third parties are being used that do not appear on approved vendor lists and have not been subject to due diligence, if reimbursements related to gifts, travel, and entertainment are being made within pre-authorized levels with supporting documentation and otherwise in a way that is inconsistent with company policies, or if other key processes are not being followed.

Forensic Accounting Review. Companies can confirm that they are not disbursing money in ways not anticipated by conducting diagnostics of their books and records to test for suspicious transactions. For example, they can review the general ledger for potential improper payments in high-risk transactions. If a particular employee oversees frequent transactions with government officials, his or her expense accounts can be reviewed. If a particular service provider is a common intermediary between the company and the government, payments to it can be checked. Companies can review accounts related to "consultants," "entertainment," "agent fees," or "commissions" for unusual patterns or entries. They can look at petty cash to ensure that it is not being used for off-the-books payments. Internal audit or external forensic specialists can provide the best support for these reviews.

How Small- and Medium-Sized Enterprises Meet Compliance Expectations

Large companies are not the only ones subject to FCPA enforcement scrutiny, and they are not the only ones that should have compliance practices in place. While large multinational corporations are regularly in the crosshairs of FCPA enforcement, smaller companies can be subject to enforcement, too. For example, Dallas Airmotive, an airline repair and overhaul company with less than 1,000 employees, settled an FCPA action in 2014 for improper payments in Brazil, Peru, and Argentina.

In fact, smaller companies are often more vulnerable. They can be easy targets for bribery shakedowns, since they have lower profiles than larger companies. In a 201 survey conducted by FTI Consulting of executives at hundreds of companies operating in Mexico, 21% of respondents overall said that it was "necessary or very necessary" to pay bribes to do business with the government while 37% of executives at small companies expressed the same sentiment. Smaller companies are also more likely to go out of business as a result of an FCPA investigation. One example is Direct Access Partners, a Wall Street brokerage firm with only 30 employees that was investigated for making improper payments in Venezuela in 2013. After this investigation began, the firm closed down its business.

How should small and medium-sized enterprises ("SMEs") apply these standards, especially smaller companies that still have significant corruption risk profiles? SMEs' resources, personnel, and capacity are usually much more limited than those of multinational corporations. Does a privately held oil and gas services company with 100 employees in Texas and 250 on-site in Brazil need a stand-alone compliance officer? How robust of a third-party due diligence and monitoring program does a small technology company with 200 distributors throughout Latin America need to have in place? These are the types of questions that companies need to answer for themselves.

To seek answers to their questions, SMEs may want to refer to the following helpful materials and sources:

U.S. Sentencing Guidelines. Section 8B2.1 of the U.S. Sentencing Guidelines provides a description of compliance expectations for smaller companies, explaining that SMEs "shall demonstrate the same degree of commitment to ethical conduct and compliance with the law as large organizations." It states that SMEs can meet these requirements with "less formality and fewer resources" than larger companies. This can mean reliance on existing resources or systems that are simpler than those of larger companies.

The Sentencing Guidelines provide four examples:

➢ The governing authority's discharge of its responsibility for oversight of the compliance and ethics program by directly managing the organization's compliance and ethics efforts;

➢ Training employees through informal staff meetings, and monitoring through regular "walk-arounds" or continuous observation while managing the organization;

➤ Using available personnel, rather than employing separate staff, to carry out the compliance and ethics program; and

➤ Modeling its own compliance and ethics program on existing, well-regarded compliance and ethics programs and best practices of other similar organizations.

FCPA Resource Guide. The FCPA Resource Guide provides, "small- and medium-size enterprises likely will have different compliance programs from large multi-national corporations, a fact DOJ and SEC take into account when evaluating companies' compliance programs." Chuck Duross, who headed the DOJ's FCPA Unit from 2010 to 2014, once explained that one of the main reasons for producing the FCPA Resource Guide was to help provide information for smaller companies: "In October 2010 the OECD proposed that we provide better guidance as to both our enforcement priorities, our interpretations of the statute and the like, particularly aimed towards small and medium enterprises ... the guide was the ultimate product of that." This insight suggests that Chapter Five of the FCPA Resource Guide's description of the "Hallmarks of Effective Compliance Programs" should be read, understood, and followed not only by multinational corporations, but by SMEs, as well.

Enforcement officials. The Assistant Director of the SEC's FCPA Unit, Charles Cain, and former Chief of the DOJ's Fraud Section, Jeffrey Knox, have discussed SMEs in the context of FCPA enforcement. Cain noted that, while the SEC recognizes that companies have different resources, smaller companies still need to find ways to manage risk:

I can't give specific examples how, but it generally involves the creative use of existing resources. While not the same as big companies, they are addressing the same risks and need to be creative. They need to make it a standard part of business. If compliance is part of the culture, the compliance program overlay doesn't need to be as big.

Knox noted that authorities would still ask, "Were the [compliance] actions taken reasonable? Was there management involvement? Was the misconduct pervasive? What is the culture of the company?"

In 2014, the SEC's Kara Brockmeyer noted that smaller companies need compliance mechanisms in place, but that they do not necessarily need "Rolls-Royce" programs. She advised that SMEs should still try to leverage the controls they have in place to address FCPA risks. For example, SMEs should use their internal audit function to ensure books and records are complete, supporting documentation is maintained for expenditures, employees know what they can spend money on, and segregation of duties and authorization levels are in place. She said that the types of controls that help prevent misconduct like embezzlement are the same controls that can prevent bribery.

In 2014, Patrick Stokes also explained that the DOJ realizes that SMEs cannot conduct the same type of M&A due diligence as larger companies. But he said, "We expect them to identify the highest risk areas and take a look at the books and some contracts to the extent possible and follow it up and conduct more thorough review of various subsidiary and units around the world where it is operating."

When to Use Outside Help for FCPA Compliance Matters

Given that Latin America presents considerable corruption risks, and anti-corruption compliance in the region can become complicated, companies often find it necessary to look for outside help. External lawyers, accountants, technology consultants, due diligence and investigation groups, and providers of online training programs all play critical roles in helping companies build anti-corruption compliance programs throughout the region. Increasingly in the region, local service providers are building impressive capabilities in these areas to support the compliance programs of companies operating in the region. They provide "home grown" solutions for Latin American businesses. But companies should know when to use them.

Before seeking outside assistance, companies should implement the following basic measures:

Assign responsibility. Outside compliance experts are of little help if there is not a person at the company in charge of directing and overseeing their work. When outside providers take direction from multiple people, communication lines can become crossed. Bills can quickly add up. Whether it is the general counsel or a specific compliance officer, companies are wise to appoint one person with responsibility for managing compliance enhancements.

Ensure broad-based commitment. The board and management should understand what compliance enhancements will entail. They should be informed of the things that will be expected of the company as the program is built. They should also have a sense of what a compliant company will ultimately look like. Without up-front commitment, companies can waste time and resources. For example, situations occur where experts are well into conducting a risk assessment and designing a program when a senior officer suddenly decides to pull the plug. Such actions might even create greater risk for the company. Imagine how enforcement officials would perceive a company that takes initial steps to better understand its risks and enhance its program, and then suddenly decides to stop.

Have a comprehensive plan. A "scattershot" approach to compliance can be a waste of time and resources. All too often, companies hire outside help in ways that are not timely, are misdirected, and might even undermine ultimate compliance objectives. A company should not hastily hire experts to conduct FCPA training in an operational area of concern when its policies on which to train are outdated. A company should not decide to design and roll out a due diligence program before employees understand why they need to prioritize this work or before they are equipped to interpret the data obtained. For example, it is harder to build controls on an *ad hoc* basis around specific instances of gifts, entertainment, and hospitality, instead of developing a broad policy to guide such interactions when they arise. Instead, companies should use outside assistance pursuant to a comprehensive approach, analyzing where they currently are, where they need to be, and creating a roadmap to reach this goal. Enforcement officials want to know that a company has a plan for meeting basic compliance expectations, and they want to see evidence that the company is advancing pursuant to that plan. By seeking outside assistance pursuant to a comprehensive plan, companies help ensure they can achieve maximum value for their investment of resources.

Do your homework. Before a company starts spending its compliance dollars, it should take some time to do its homework. Ample amounts of publicly available information exist that can assist companies in improving their compliance programs. One helpful starting point is to reach out to industry peers to understand how they approach compliance. Benchmarking against other companies can be essential. Seeking recommendations can save time.

———

It is all too easy for a company to want to apply the exact same compliance policies, procedures, strategies, and methodologies to its Latin American operations as it does in other parts of the world. But a template approach can lead to lack of effectiveness—and if compliance efforts are ineffective, resources go to waste, and corruption risk still persist. To be effective on the ground, it is essential for companies to think critically about unique risks and compliance needs in the region and to tailor their approaches accordingly. A thoughtful approach is the best protection.

Chapter 6

Where Culture Fits Into Compliance in Latin America

One of the bedrock lessons from the FCPA is that, when it comes to enforcement, cultural norms are irrelevant. It does not matter to law enforcement officials whether corrupt acts—like paying "commissions" to sales agents in Brazil, giving a "tip" to a highway official in Mexico, or hiring the unqualified son of the Colombian Minister of Mines—are standard practice in a certain country. Yes, it is true that the FCPA provides an affirmative defense for activity that is lawful under written local laws or regulations. But written laws in Latin America never legalize bribery, not even petty corruption. In this way, FCPA attorneys and those responsible for enforcement often must ignore cultural practices.

But when considering anti-corruption compliance, the situation is just the opposite. Recognizing the importance of local culture can be key, especially in Latin America. If companies do not respond to local norms in structuring their programs, companies will not be able to effectively convey compliance concepts and manage corruption risk. Companies in Latin America are using cultural cues to tailor compliance strategies in a variety of different ways.

The "Circle of Trust" in Compliance

Successful compliance officers in Latin America regularly say that the most important lesson for the development of an effective compliance program is to establish positive relationships with business units in a company. Patrick Henz, compliance officer for the Americas at Primetals Technologies, describes the need to establish a "circle of trust." Weatherford's Regional Compliance Counsel for Latin America, Marco Padilla, similarly explains the relationship as one that must be built on confidence, where employees feel that they and their company will be better off if employees disclose an issue than if they do not. Thus, he says, a compliance officer must be a "trusted business partner." Compliance works best in Latin America when relationships are collaborative, not static.

If, on the other hand, the compliance officer is seen as a threat, the compliance function runs the risk of breaking down. Employees might not seek out guidance when there is an issue of potential compliance significance. Even worse, they might choose to hide certain transactions to avoid potential scrutiny – even if the transactions are entirely legitimate – undermining a culture of transparency. There can also be an unintended reverse effect when employees, who are prone to engage in criminal acts, feel more compelled to actually engage in them because of the wall that exists between a company's rule-enforcing employees and its business-generating personnel.

If unaddressed, the divide can grow into hostility. In one situation, an outsider from the United States was brought into a Mexican company to build compliance measures, and began his work by requiring employees to participate in a two-day "introduction" workshop on anti-corruption laws. The trainer spoke only in English and showed no interest in establishing a personal rapport with the employees. On day two, the employees showed up wearing Mexican soccer team jerseys. When the trainer asked if Mexico was playing that day, the employees laughed. They had worn the jerseys as a display of defiance to the out-of-touch newcomer, who many associated with "Yankee Imperialism," a historical attitude toward aggressive United States intrusion in Mexican affairs. This small episode illustrates that, in Latin America, local norms must be acknowledged if a compliance officer wants her efforts to be worthwhile. Without showing respect, compliance will falter.

Compliance officers need to become trusted partners of the business units. They need to be seen as resources for guidance and support. How does one build a circle of trust in Latin America? How does one foster true buy-in?

Some common best practices are discussed below.

Make the personal touch. Some compliance officers in the region go out of their ways to make the personal touch. They have personal sit-downs and go to coffees with employees and make site-visits to company units away from headquarters. They may also do so with business partners by scheduling in-person visits in which they describe in detail the company's compliance program. They may explain to the third-party the nature of indirect liability to demonstrate why the very existence of the engagement creates a risk. Making a personal effort to explain the laws and trends behind compliance facilitates a cooperative relationship.

One compliance officer tells the story about how keeping a bowl of candy on her desk and her office door wide open results in her colleagues regularly dropping by to chat, which can serve to strengthen the compliance function. Another compliance officer tells how his in-person meeting with one employee actually inspired the employee to make a presentation on ethics at the local university. In Latin America, face-to-face engagement can go a long way.

Ensure empowerment. Red tape is a common feature of Latin American business, and it is all too easy for a compliance officer to fall into the trap of being perceived as merely another formality. One way companies avoid this perception is by empowering compliance officers to act in meaningful ways. Rather than serving as one more checkpoint in a company bureaucracy, compliance personnel can be given a leadership voice in the organization. Compliance officers can make determinations on when policy violations occur. They can be given the ability to stop a high-risk transaction from going forward, or at least be provided a strong voice to influence executives who make the final call.

Emphasize local laws. Any employee of a company subject to the FCPA can create liability for the company by paying bribes, no matter how far away from the United States the employee resides. The problem is that the further away from the United States the employee sits, the more abstract, foreign, and insignificant the FCPA can seem. How does a company emphasize the importance of FCPA compliance for those situated far from headquarters? One way is by educating employees about local anti-corruption laws in compliance policies, guidelines, and trainings.

Make trainings "local." Compliance trainings are more effective when they incorporate local cultural considerations and are conducted in local languages. For example, by role-playing corruption scenarios that commonly occur in a specific country, employees can better understand the dynamics of compliance. Brazilian employees can be shown, in Portuguese, what to do when an official asks for *uma propina* ("a tip"). Mexican teams can be trained on how to handle a *mordida* ("a bite") request from the electricity company. Such education and training will help employees better grasp expectations and rules.

Be sensitive to cultural concerns of acquired companies. After a corporate acquisition, acquiring companies generally want to quickly integrate new companies into their compliance programs, but sometimes they need to take time to respond to cultural considerations. One colleague was embedded in an acquired company for six months to manage the FCPA compliance integration of the formerly family-run business. The local company needed to be brought up to speed quickly on compliance processes. The colleague recognized that she could not have done her job successfully without a high degree of cultural sensitivity. This meant she was able to listen to local employees more often than dictating to them, to know when to introduce new compliance concepts and correct lingering mis-understandings (and when not to do so), to sense when to concede issues and when to push back, and to artfully generate buy-in from the company's various sectors. It meant first building respect and trust through personal relationships, in ling dinners and family gatherings with her local colleagues. It also meant slowly educating the company on the stakes associated with non-compliance and the rationale behind the rules. After six months, the local company was up to speed and had internalized the compliance processes in a way it would not have if compliance would have been one-way mandated.

Focusing on Values

While in some parts of the world a rules-based compliance program may work best, programs in Latin America seem to work better when they emphasize values instead.

Of course rules must always be part of a compliance program, and a rules-based approach does provide obvious benefits. For one, it establishes clear guidelines on what laws must be followed and is often more efficient to enforce. Latin American personnel, however, often respond best when, above all else, they know that programs are part of the fabric of the organization, woven into the company's DNA. Employees respond more positively to matters concerning business ethics and personal morals. Programs work better when employees feel emotionally connected to protecting a company's reputation for conducting clean and transparent business. Employees gain a feeling of pride when their companies succeed based on working hard and competing fairly in the marketplace, not by cutting corners and engaging in corrupt acts. Appealing to employees to "do the right thing" also helps generate ownership in compliance throughout an organization.

Moreover, in Latin America, when a company loses its good reputation, employees often feel the effects directly. When a company makes headlines for engaging in corrupt activity, it tarnishes the company's name and, with it, the reputation of all its employees. In this way, employees often have a personal reason for wanting to protect a company's reputation.

Another reason why a values-based approach works so well in Latin America is because employees are often less swayed by written rules, which might be connected to the lax enforcement of laws on the books in many parts of the region. Lax enforcement has resulted in high levels of perceived impunity. In the 2016 Latin American Corruption Survey, only about half of the respondents from the region thought that an offender is likely to be prosecuted in the country where they work. When the consequences of violating laws are amorphous, employees come to believe that it is irrelevant to follow policies designed to comply with those laws. Telling employees that they must follow company policy or risk going to jail has little impact in jurisdictions where people rarely go to jail for corruption-related offenses.

In practice, best-in-class companies in Latin America estab-lish values-based compliance programs in various ways. Examples of those measures are described below.

> **The value of ethics is reinforced by a strong tone-from-the-top.** The CEO regularly makes public statements stressing the importance of the ethics and compliance program and sends e-mail reminders on a quarterly basis, recapping compliance success stories and instilling in business unit leaders that they own compliance risk. Additionally, senior-level executives, including the CEO, help lead annual staff-wide compliance trainings.

> **Compliance has a seat at the table.** Compliance is involved in business decisions from the start, rather than being brought in at the last minute. For example, compliance officers participate in board meetings, with an active role in sharing data related to areas of risk with decision makers.

> **The company takes a collaborative approach to compliance.** Designated "compliance champions" from various business units (often appointed by their peers) engage in monthly "compliance meet-ups," in which they gather to discuss com-pliance challenges or creative ideas for program modification. Additionally, compliance officers themselves regularly seek input from business unit leaders, demonstrating a collabora-tive approach to the program.

> **Companies rotate compliance officers in and out of busi-ness units.** This helps facilitate better relationships between the compliance teams and the business units, and further encourages business unit leaders to take on ownership of

compliance. Often, business leaders have the ability to spread a much stronger message about compliance than those who have responsibility for only compliance, who sometimes are perceived as a company's internal police officers.

➢ **Compliance leaders interact with industry peers.** Compliance officers attend industry conferences where they showcase the strength of their company's compliance program to the business community. This, in turn, helps to generate a sense of pride among employees about their company's culture of ethics and compliance.

➢ **The company regularly instills the importance of ethical behavior.** The company establishes a set of guiding principles that form the backbone of its Codes of Conduct and Business Ethics. Some companies take it a step further by creating a summarized version of their principles, posting them in lunchrooms and hallways. By creating a summarized version, too, employees can carry handouts and distribute them at meetings with government officials, subcontractors, business partners, and other contacts with whom company personnel interact. Furthermore, managers and supervisors give regular reminders at monthly staff meetings on the importance of compliance and ethics.

➢ **Compliance metrics are embedded in performance reviews.** Managers and supervisors include compliance metrics in performance reviews, with input from the compliance department, so that compensation, promotion, and bonuses incorporate a commitment to compliance. This gives employees concrete incentives to pay attention to compliance.

> **Positive behavior is recognized and rewarded.** Companies find ways to honor personnel who have contributed to the compliance program in a positive way. For example, the employee may be brought to headquarters to meet with the CEO, be publically recognized in the company's online newsletter, or be rewarded during a "town hall" ceremony.

> **Bad behavior is handled appropriately.** Employees who engage in misconduct are swiftly disciplined. Such disciplinary measures can include termination for serious violations, no matter the employee's position in the company.

When first introducing an anti-corruption compliance program in Latin America, achieving local buy-in can be a challenge. People might be accustomed to doing things a certain way. Sometimes corporate culture must change to make compliance efforts work. Such change is not something that happens overnight, but it can be generated most quickly when companies know how to appeal to their employees' values.

Appealing to Emotion

On Mexican highways, there are official government signs that read, "*Conduce con precaución. Tu familia te espera*" ("Drive carefully. Your family is waiting for you"), and "*Después de un accidente, ya nada es igual*" ("After an accident, nothing is the same"). On some routes, the government might leave wreckage from car accidents with signs that read, "In January 2013, six people died here." In this way, the government seeks to convince people to drive safely by appealing to emotion. In fact, emotion is a common driver of action in Latin America in many ways. It is on display in television advertisements and news reporting. The most popular soccer commentators are the ones that scream, weep, and holler. In these ways, Latin American audiences are affected by messages that impact their hearts.

This dynamic has relevance for anti-corruption compliance programs as well. Incorporating an emotional element into compliance efforts can make compliance work better. One compliance officer in Mexico, for example, begins her trainings by discussing the types of leaders they wish to have in Mexico, the pride they feel when their leaders do the right thing and the shame that results when they do not. An Argentine compliance leader likes to ask about people's families and children when training on compliance procedures. He asks: "Is a corrupt business environment the type of place we really want to leave to our kids?" One Colombian company plans to produce a compliance video that shows a non-compliant executive being arrested by U.S. authorities upon arrival in Miami en route to Disney World, while his children look on with tears in their eyes.

Invoking emotion plays off of values, including family and pride. It focuses on how people ultimately relate to one another. It motivates people at the core. This is often how the most fundamental change in corporate behavior occurs, especially in Latin America.

Cultural Nuances in Internal Reporting Mechanisms

Internal reporting mechanisms, such as confidential and anonymous hotlines, offer employees a way to report potential anti-corruption violations. FCPA enforcement officials expect such mechanisms as standard components of compliance programs. Companies seeking to implement them in Latin America, however, need to consider a number of issues, including what types of technology to use, how to train employees to use it, and how to handle reports when they come in.

To ensure that hotline programs work successfully in Latin America, companies often make the following adaptations:

Incorporate local culture and language. To make hotlines and other reporting mechanisms credible in the eyes of Latin American audiences, companies publicize them in local languages with local idioms. A company working in Brazil should not hire a Portuguese provider to draft its Brazilian hotline materials with Portugal terminology. These messages must be communicated in local fashions and by local providers. This includes putting posters in common areas of businesses where employees regularly congregate. One Colombian company likes to publish cartoons on its intranet reminding employees of the ways they can report violations.

Clearly explain the hotline's purpose. When educating the Latin American workforce on internal reporting mechanisms, companies should take extra care to explain the specific *purpose* of the hotline: to find out about potential corruption. If not, a hotline can be perceived as a way of expressing all sorts of opinions and grievances to their company. Although workers may report potential anti-corruption violations, they may also feel compelled to disclose a host of other issues, for example, that their boss leaves work early, their colleagues chat by the printer, or they were passed over for a promotion. This can overwhelm hotlines with reports that have nothing to do with bribery or corruption. One Venezuelan compliance officer once complained that his tip line had turned into a *telenovela* (what we refer to in the United States as a "soap opera"). To maximize the effectiveness of the hotline, employees must understand what is appropriate and what is not.

Clearly explain the hotline's process. As important as it is to explain to employees the purpose of the hotline, it is equally important for employees to have accurate expectations about how reports into the hotline will be used. Employees should understand, for example, that they should not expect to receive a final report concerning the findings. At the same time, however, when an employee has a credible tip, it is important for the company to keep the person apprised of progress in the internal review. This demonstrates to employees that the company is taking reports seriously and reduces the potential that the employee will take the same information to law enforcement, either in that country or in the United States.

Stress anti-retaliation protections. In many Latin American countries, employees might have a sincere and reasonable reluctance to come forward with reports of corruption. In countries like Honduras or Argentina, such reluctance might be due to a genuine fear for personal safety, or a lack of faith in the courts to protect them. In other countries like Paraguay or Bolivia, such reluctance might be due to the fact that, if an employee who makes the report is terminated as a result, it might be hard for that employee to find another job given the lack of local employment opportunities. To overcome this reluctance, companies should make continuous efforts to stress that hotlines are anonymous and that the company maintains a zero-tolerance policy toward any form of retaliation. Companies may also want to give employees the option of submitting tips by e-mail or other methods, since some employees might fear that hotlines tips could be recorded and traced.

Appoint qualified hotline personnel. The people who manage hotlines and other reporting mechanisms, including those who listen and respond to reports, should be well-trained and familiar with local cultural nuances. Having a call center in New Jersey for a report from Nicaragua is not the most effective structure. The people who receive the calls should be able to engage with callers according to local customs and norms. They should also be prepared to be good listeners, to ask open-ended questions, and to respond to complaints in ways that avoid creating unnecessary legal exposure for the company, a particularly difficult task given the strong labor protections in many Latin American countries. As a result, hotline personnel also should have a basic familiarity of local labor rules.

Regional managers and ethics offices should have similar familiarity, since another common way in which violations are reported is through these personnel. Managers are the eyes and ears on the ground and often are the best conduits for reminding employees of their reporting options. Nor is it uncommon for managers to directly receive sensitive reports of compliance issues. For these reasons, managers should be educated on how to handle reports when they come in. If the company is highly decentralized, it should have an ethics officer at each operational unit throughout the region tasked with handling complaints. Systems must be designed to educate all actors in the reporting chain about which issues to escalate and how to track reports. Mechanisms should be in place to ensure documentation and tracking of the reports.

— • —

Those best positioned to inject Latin American cultural norms into compliance are from local communities themselves. They can more easily identify relevant practices and opportunities to "tropicalize" compliance, as the process is referred to locally in the region. However, companies should always be careful not to be overly reliant on these local efforts – the concept of "culture" can sometimes be used as an excuse for promoting lax controls, too. When a local Brazilian company tells you there is no such thing as a "forensic accounting" discipline in the country, or that it is inconsistent with local culture to vet the books and records of a business partner in a critical way for corruption issues when exercising audit rights, the "culture" rationale should be suspect. In these cases, practitioners should demand adherence to international compliance standards, not purported local practices.

Chapter 7

Managing Third-Party Relationships in Latin America

Perhaps the most important component of anti-corruption compliance in Latin America is managing the risk of indirect bribery payments. Under the FCPA, a company can be held liable when its agents, consultants, distributors, lawyers, accountants, customs brokers, or any other intermediary makes payments to foreign officials on its behalf. Liability arises if the company or individual knows that the third party will make the payment, authorizes the third party to do so, consciously disregards red flags suggesting the possibility of corrupt payments, or (for publicly listed companies in the United States) fails to put in place controls designed to prevent third-party bribes.

Between the late 1990s and the end of 2015, the majority of FCPA actions involving bribery in Latin America included the participation of third parties. Third parties played a role in more than 75% of the cases covering payments in Argentina, almost 60% of the cases covering payments in Brazil, and more than 65% of the cases covering payments in Mexico. FCPA enforcement officials announced publicly in 2013 that, more generally, 70% of FCPA actions in the prior two years had involved third-party payments. In 2014, the OECD Foreign Bribery Report stated that, since 1999, three out of four cases in the world involved the participation of intermediaries, including subsidiary companies.

Building third-party due diligence programs can be a particularly daunting task in Latin America. For one, companies in the region tend to rely heavily on non-employees to support their work, some even using thousands of consultants, agents, distributors, suppliers, and other third parties. In some cases, legal systems require the use of third parties. For example, Mexican customs regulations mandate that certain documentation be prepared and processed by a licensed Mexican customs broker. In other countries, a company cannot appear in court without a lawyer.

Given the complex nature of regulatory regimes in many Latin American countries, companies often seek a third party's expertise for services such as calculating tax liabilities or applying for an environmental impact permit. The *gestor* ("manager") in Mexico, *despachante* ("dispatcher") in Brazil, and local fixers and processors in other countries are well-established professions, because they can navigate regulatory mazes and are often on a first name basis with officials who sit behind government office windows.

Moreover, interpersonal relationships in the region are usually essential to business, which puts a premium on consultants and agents who are well connected to help find valuable business opportunities and accomplish tasks quicker. This is especially the case in economies with high levels of market concentration, where a small and insulated group of people controls levers of economic and government power. As a result, business people are compelled to use consultants who have a network of valuable relationships, even if their technical expertise is questionable. Sometimes these consultants are former government officials and know how to navigate opaque systems of influence. A construction company in Argentina might legitimately want to retain the services of a former military official, for example, who knows how to obtain permits for use of explosives. An energy company understandably might seek out a former Pemex official to help with preparing bidding documentation with nuanced requirements. Because government officials in Latin America typically do not wait long after leaving office to represent entities before the same government agencies, consultants with this type of pedigree are common.

Sometimes companies feel pressure to use sales agents and distributors because they open the door to the only viable sales channel in a country. For example, a pharmaceutical company that is new to Brazil may find it difficult to distribute its products throughout the country unless it can rely on distribution networks already in place. Similarly, a company trying to sell food products in Mexico might find that certain regions' retail networks are controlled by monopolies that require sales to be made indirectly through intermediaries.

Adding to the challenge is the fact that companies might not even detect that a particular third party creates FCPA risk. This may occur when a service provider in the region offers a variety of services not directly related to its core business. In stagnant economies, providers often will look for ways to broaden their business. Take as an example, a travel agent in Bolivia who happens to be performing other non-traditional tasks, like obtaining government health certifications for employees. This phenomenon can make it difficult for companies to monitor vendor master lists, identify providers engaged in higher risk activities, and target their due diligence efforts accordingly.

Companies might also find it challenging for their compliance teams to manage effective due diligence programs for the simple reason that not every third party with whom a company associates requires the same level of due diligence, and choosing the appropriate level of due diligence to perform on a particular intermediary is often an uncertain exercise. This fact tends not to sit well with individuals accustomed to civil law systems, where detailed legal codes spell out specific rules for specific situations and laws are less frequently left to interpretation. Moreover, because the need to conduct third-party due diligence usually flows from liability under U.S. law, namely the FCPA, and not liability under local laws, it may be a formidable challenge to persuade Latin American employees to take third-party due diligence seriously.

Nevertheless, it appears that more companies in the region are starting to take steps to manage corruption risks associated with their third party relationships. In the Latin America Corruption

Survey conducted in 2012, 32% of respondents working at local and regional companies said that their companies performed third party due diligence, a rate that went up to 49% when the survey was conducted in 2016. For respondents from multinational companies, the percentage went up from 60 to 66 during the same time period. While 30% of respondents from local and regional companies said in 2016 that their companies perform due diligence on acquisition targets and merger partners, that percentage was 50 for multinational companies. These numbers suggest a growing sophistication on the part of Latin American companies toward managing third party corruption risks.

Mitigating Third-Party Risk

Many factors create a heightened need for companies in Latin America to focus resources and attention on managing their third-party relationships. Companies can take a variety of steps when developing due diligence and monitoring strategies. The strategies that a company will deploy in each case will depend on a wide range of factors, including levels of risks, specific circumstances, and the nature of specific relationships.

Prior to engaging in a third-party relationship, companies should consider the following steps:

➢ Request references from the third party's customers and business associates.

➢ Require the third party to complete a questionnaire about its beneficial ownership, license and registration statuses, business history, history of criminal or other unlawful activity, business profile, qualifications, internal compliance or ethics program, and financial health.

➢ Obtain documentation from the third party—such as relevant bank documents, background employment information from relevant third party personnel, incorporation documents, licenses, and permits, to establish the entity's qualifications and legitimacy.

➢ Conduct due diligence on the entity by performing online searches and reviews against international and local denied party lists.

➢ Commission a due diligence review from a professional provider that can be conducted with varying degrees of depth, from online searches to field investigations and verifications, to discrete inquiries.

➢ Conduct interviews with third party personnel to understand its risk profile and clarify any outstanding factual uncertainties related to the due diligence review.

➢ Establish and document the reasonableness of the third party's fees or compensation structure based on market rates—and, in higher risk situations, seek fixed-fee or hourly-based fee arrangements instead of success fees.

➢ Establish a work plan or similar proposal that describes in detail the specific services the third party will provide.

➢ Obtain a copy of the third party's compliance policies, or require that the third party adopt an anti-corruption compliance program itself if it does not already have one.

➢ Require prior notice for the third party's contact with government officials.

➢ Conduct compliance training of relevant third-party personnel.

After the third-party is vetted, companies should consider the following:

➢ Document the business justification for use of each third party.

➢ Assign a business sponsor tasked with overseeing monitoring of the third party who is responsible for the relationship who can recognize FCPA risks.

➢ Conduct periodic reviews of the third party's books and records related to its services for the company.

➢ Require the third party to complete an annual anti-corruption compliance certification.

➢ Train the third party's personnel on compliance on an annual basis.

Companies may also want to include contractual representations, warranties, and procedures in a written agreement with the intermediary to address compliance issues. For example, they should require the intermediary to agree to anti-corruption compliance commitments under both the FCPA and local law. Detailed audit rights, written in a broad way to encompass review of expense reports and interviews with relevant intermediary employees, give companies the ability to follow up if they see any indicators of potential bribery violations or other corruption. Audit rights should also be specific, such as in specifying that the company shall be the one to define the scope of the audit and select the auditors. If audit rights are not drafted carefully, companies in Latin American jurisdictions might be left with access to tax and accounting books only.

Contractual provisions should also be drafted to prohibit the intermediary from subcontracting to subagents, a common practice in the region, without the express consent of the company. Further, these provisions should prohibit intermediaries from giving gifts or incurring hospitality expenses on behalf of work for the company.

Termination clauses can help companies extricate themselves from engagements if there are indicators that the intermediary engaged in corrupt payments. These provisions should be as specific as possible to ensure they are valid under local laws in Latin America. For example, if a company does not specify that it can immediately terminate an agreement, at the company's sole discretion if it has reason to believe the third party violated anti-corruption laws, a local court might require a final judicial decision on the issue before the contract can be terminated. This would leave the company in the position of breaching a contract (with potentially severe penalties and the likelihood that it would be prevented from contracting with another third party) or continuing in a relationship that could subject it to criminal violations.

Since local intermediaries in the region do not always maintain detailed books and records of all transactions, companies will want to require them to keep complete records of this engagement, based on international standards. The records they should keep should specifically include employee expense reports, backup support, and petty cash, as well as e-mails of employees working on the company's matters. The agreement should further require that they maintain the files for at least five years, the statute of limitations that applies to FCPA violations.

Although these examples are common ways in which companies manage risk that their third parties will pay bribes on their behalf, the exact safeguards that a company applies should reflect the levels of risk each third party creates.

As with all areas of anti-corruption compliance, companies should maintain complete and well-organized records of their due diligence efforts. Tom Fox is known to say that the three most important words in compliance are "document, document, and document."

Determining the Scope of Third-Party Due Diligence

How deep must a company dig when engaging a third-party intermediary? How much third party anti-corruption due diligence is enough? There are no easy answers to these questions, since they ultimately must be determined on a case-by-case basis. Such uncertainties can create particular challenges in Latin America, since

Latin American companies tend to operate best when they have a clear and explicit interpretation of what the laws require of them. In practice, many factors are at play in each determination, and different companies have different risk tolerances in devising internal third party due diligence policies. The levels of fair, reasonable, and adequate due diligence are highly dependent on context. As a result, FCPA compliance professionals are prone to say, "It depends." They add, "Enforcers won't tell you."

In fact, third-party due diligence requires a careful balancing act. On one hand, a company does not want to do too much, because it can throttle the business. On the other hand, doing too little will make the company vulnerable. Thus, many companies settle on "a happy medium."

The DOJ and the SEC explain in the FCPA Resource Guide that, when vetting third parties, companies should take into consideration several factors, including their qualifications, business reputations, relationships with foreign officials, and the business rationale for their use. Due diligence should be heightened when red flags are present.

Above and beyond the considerations mentioned above, companies also should follow these basic principles when conducting third-party due diligence:

Keep it risk-based. Not all third parties require the same degree of due diligence. A company's sales agent in Argentina will require a deeper level of review than its transportation service provider in Uruguay. Its freight forwarder in Ecuador will need more scrutiny than the company that cleans the office in Chile. The FCPA Resource Guide states, "Risk-based due diligence is particularly important with third parties and will also be considered by DOJ and SEC in assessing the effectiveness of a company's compliance program." In taking a risk-based approach, many companies classify their third parties based on factors like industry, geographic location, size, and the nature of the transaction. These companies apply a tiered system for reviews depending on where a third party falls on the risk spectrum. Within a specific transaction, a company might further refine its due diligence needs depending on specific risk issues that arise over time. In short, companies should have a plan in place to address low, medium, and high-risk situations.

Ensure that it makes sense. The reasoning behind a company's third-party due diligence program should make sense, not only to those charged with implementing it, but also to enforcement officials. The more complex the program, the harder it will be to implement. When due diligence programs are guided by an overriding logic, companies are able to explain to enforcement officials the matter under review in the context of all of their efforts if something happens to go wrong. One way that companies can demonstrate the reasonableness of their programs is by benchmarking them against what other companies are doing in the same sector or industry. Thus, gaining familiarity about other companies' actions (particularly in the same sector) can be extremely helpful, both in formulating a company's programs and in defending it.

Apply it consistently. If a third party within a particular risk category is subject to an in-country review of its public records, and another third party in the same category is not, such inconsistent treatment could raise questions. Exceptions to an overall rule might be necessary, but the reasoning behind them should be sensible and well documented.

Companies should be able to demonstrate their due diligence practices years after they review a third party. To achieve this, they must keep records of the steps taken and information obtained. Records should be kept on not only the third parties with which they engage, but also the ones they choose not to hire. In this way, companies can demonstrate that they have robust compliance programs.

It is a common misconception that large and established third parties in Latin America do not have to be properly vetted. Although unknown agents and consultants in foreign territories create obvious risk under the FCPA, large and established third-party intermediaries and their employees can just as easily violate anti-corruption laws. In fact, several companies have wound up under scrutiny by FCPA officials for the corrupt acts of their "large and established" third parties. For example, Baker Hughes settled with the SEC in 2001 to resolve allegations that the Indonesian affiliate of KPMG, a well-known accounting firm, bribed Indonesian officials to reduce a subsidiary's tax liability. The SEC accordingly increased the company's penalty by US$10 million for violating the terms of this settlement during Baker Hughes's second encounter with the FCPA in 2007. Several oil exploration, production, and services companies—Pride International, Tidewater Marine, Transocean, and Shell, to name a few—used the well-known Swiss freight-forwarder, Panalpina, only to learn that the firm was making payments to customs officials in

Nigeria on their behalves. Vetting the local Latin American operations of global third-party providers is especially important, because these local units might not share the same reputations or control structures as headquarters. They might also rely on local partners, who might, themselves, engage in wrongdoing.

Another common misconception in Latin America is that a company does not need to vet its lawyers. Perhaps they assume that lawyers are lower risk, since lawyers are usually bound by stricter codes of ethics and can usually lose their license to practice if they engage in corruption. But, by their very nature, certain roles for lawyers pose high risk, such as when they serve as intermediaries with regulatory or judicial officials, including judges. For example, the medical devices company, Stryker Corporation, paid the SEC US$13.2 million in penalties in 2013, in part because the company's Mexican subsidiary used a Mexican law firm as a conduit for a US$46,000 improper payment to Mexican officials so the company could retain a contract. Wal-Mart's lawyers in Mexico were also instrumental in the alleged bribery scheme there. More generally, the 2014 OECD Foreign Bribery Report concluded that six percent of foreign bribery cases worldwide since 1999 had involved lawyers. In another study conducted by the International Bar Association in 2010, half of respondents stated that corruption was an issue in the legal profession.

Common Third-Party Red Flags

Liability for a third party's actions can be based on a company's actual knowledge or constructive knowledge of the illegality of these actions. Thus, as part of their third-party due diligence and monitoring programs, companies are expected to train their workforces to recognize "red flags" that may indicate that the third parties they use are engaging in corrupt acts. While the existence of a red flag does not automatically preclude the use of a specific third party, it does warrant a closer review of the entity and perhaps the application of additional controls to the relationship, thereby safeguarding against a potential FCPA violation.

Reputational Risk

☐ The transaction takes place, or the third party is located, in a country known for widespread corruption, as measured by Transparency International's Corruption Perceptions Index (CPI), or other similar indices.

☐ The third party has a history of improper payment practices, indicated by prior convictions, or ongoing, formal or informal investigations by law enforcement authorities.

☐ The third party has been subject to criminal or civil enforcement actions for acts suggesting illegal, improper, or unethical conduct

☐ The third party has a poor business reputation.

☐ The third party allegedly made or has a propensity to make prohibited payments or facilitation payments to officials.

☐ The third party has questionable integrity, such as a reputation for illegal, improper, or unethical conduct.

☐ The third party does not have in place an adequate compliance program or Code of Conduct, or refuses to adopt one.

☐ Other companies have terminated the third party for improper conduct.

☐ Information provided about the third party or its services is not verifiable by data, only anecdotally.

Government Relationships

- The third party has a family relationship, or business relationship, with a foreign official or government agency.

- The third party previously worked in the government at a high level, or in an agency relevant to the work s/he will be performing.

- The third party is a company with an owner, major shareholder or executive manager, who is a government official.

- The third party is rumored to have an undisclosed beneficial owner.

- The third party makes large or frequent political contributions.

- A government official requests, urges, insists, or demands that a particular party, company, or individual be selected or engaged, particularly if the official has discretionary authority over the business at issue.

- The third party conducts private meetings with government officials.

- The third party provides lavish gifts or hospitality to government officials.

- The third party insists on dealing with government officials without the participation of the company.

Insufficient Capabilities

- The third party is in a different line of business than that for which it has been engaged.

- The third party lacks experience or a "track record" with the product, service, field, or industry.

- The third party does not have offices or a staff, or lacks adequate facilities or staff, to perform the work.

- The third party has an unorthodox corporate structure.

- The third party is not expected to perform substantial work.

- The address of the third party's business is a mail drop location, virtual office, or small private office that could not hold a business the size that is claimed.

- The third party has not been in business for very long or was only recently incorporated.

- The third party has poor financial statements or credit.

- The third party's plan for performing the work is vague and/or suggests a reliance on contacts or relationships.

Type and Method of Compensation

- ☐ The third party requests an unusual advance payment.

- ☐ The fee, commission, or volume discount provided to the third party is unusually high compared to the market rate.

- ☐ The compensation arrangement is based on a success fee or bonus.

- ☐ The third party offers to submit, or does submit, inflated, inaccurate, or suspicious invoices.

- ☐ The third party requests an invoice to reflect a higher amount than the actual price of goods provided.

- ☐ The third party's invoice vaguely describes the services provided.

- ☐ The third party requests cash, cash equivalent, or bearer instrument payments.

- ☐ The third party requests payment in a jurisdiction outside its home country that has no relationship to the transaction or the entities involved in the transaction, especially if the country is an offshore financial center.

- ☐ The third party requests that payment be made to another third party or intermediary.

- ☐ The third party proposes the use of shell companies.

- ☐ The third party requests that payments be made to two or more accounts.

- ☐ The third party shares compensation with others whose identities are not disclosed.

- ☐ The third party requests an after-award services contract that it does not have the capacity to perform.

- ☐ The third party requests that a donation be made to a charity.

- ☐ The third party refuses to properly document expenses.

- ☐ The third party pressures the company to make the payments urgently or ahead of schedule.

- ☐ The third party requests a large advance or up-front payment.

- ☐ The third party requests payment arrangements that raise local law issues, such as payment in another country's currency.

Unusual Circumstances

- The third party refuses to agree to comply with the FCPA, the UKBA, equivalent applicable anti-corruption legislation, anti-money laundering laws, or other similar laws and regulations.

- The third party refuses to warrant past compliance with the FCPA, the UKBA, equivalent applicable anti-corruption legislation, anti-money laundering laws, or other similar laws and regulations.

- The third party refuses to execute a written contract, or requests to perform services without a written contract where one is sought.

- The third party insists that its identity remain confidential or that the relationship remain secret.

- The third party refuses to divulge the identity of its beneficial owners, directors, officers, or other principals.

- The third party refuses to answer due diligence questions.

- The third party refuses to allow audit clauses in contracts.

- A suggestion by the third party that anti-corruption compliance policies need not be followed.

- A suggestion by the third party that otherwise illegal conduct is acceptable because it is the norm or customs in a particular country.

- Suspicious statements by the third party such as needing payments to "take care of things" or "finalize the deal."

- The representation is illegal under local law.

- The alleged performance of the third party is suspiciously higher than competitors or companies in related industries.

- A third party guarantees or promises unusually high rates of return on the promotional services provided.

- The third party requests approval of a significantly excessive budget or unusual expenditures.

Responding to Third-Party Pushback

The idea of due diligence vetting is often new to local companies in Latin America that are asked to respond to questionnaires, sign compliance certifications, undergo interviews, and permit audits of their books and records. As a result, pushback by the third party can be common, even if it has nothing to hide. Thus, a request to review a Peruvian consultant's background in the local mining business may be misinterpreted as an attempt to question his knowledge and expertise, something he has worked years to perfect. Maybe a closely held Brazilian provider of customs clearance services highly values keeping its way of doing business strictly confidential, so as not to lose ground to the competition, even if its business is entirely above board.

Such reactions can be standard throughout Latin America and may cause companies doing business there to face difficult questions: What if a contractor declines to provide financial statements or *curriculum vitae* for its top sales personnel, a customs broker refuses to accept anti-corruption compliance language or audit rights in a contract, or a distributor is unwilling to describe its beneficial ownership?

Certain best practices in Latin America help companies manage these obstacles. Consider the examples below:

Teach. Companies can demonstrate to third parties why the due diligence process is necessary. They can explain that their compliance procedures apply to all business relationships, not just the one under review. They can use prior FCPA enforcement actions to show that due diligence has become an important feature of international business.

It can also help to reference other types of due diligence processes with which local companies might be more familiar, a comparison point for anti-corruption due diligence. For example, a local company might be accustomed to the "know your customer" requirements applied by financial institutions under international anti-money laundering regimes in places like Colombia and Argentina.

Listen. The third party might have a legitimate reason for refusing to accept due diligence requests. Perhaps the owners have a strategic business reason, such as a contemplated acquisition, for wanting to avoid revealing confidential business information. In booming markets throughout Latin America—including Panama, Colombia, and Peru—local companies are fast preparing themselves for potential acquisitions by international companies, which can create a desire to hold business secrets close to the vest. Perhaps the beneficial owners of an enterprise do not want their names disclosed for fear of kidnapping. Revealing detailed information in countries known for violence, like Venezuela and Mexico, could put owners' own security at risk. Given the potential for these dynamics, a company might need to do some digging to understand the underpinnings of a situation, and determine the legitimacy of responses to due diligence requests. If a third party doesn't have a valid reason for rejecting requests, this fact, in itself, could be considered a red flag.

Be flexible and willing to negotiate. Effective due diligence often requires a degree of flexibility. If a legitimate reason for the "pushback" exists, there might be other ways of obtaining the information needed. For example, companies will sometimes request the financial statements of a third party as part of the normal due diligence processes. By reviewing them, companies can confirm that the third party is a *bona fide* entity and not a shell company, a common problem in Latin America. The existence of financial statements also shows that the third party has some controls in place. Its books are probably being reviewed and approved by external auditors. In the event that a third party does not want to provide these documents, there might be other ways of accomplishing the same goals. Perhaps the company can request a reference from the third party's bank or from one of its clients as another way of conducting the review and reaching the same findings.

Stay focused on risk. FCPA enforcement officials make it very clear that third party due diligence should be tailored based on the company's unique risk profile. This means that not all third parties require the same level of review. For example, an agent that helps an oil and gas company prepare bid documentation in Mexico City to win public contracts requires a much higher level of due diligence than the company that provides office supplies for that same oil and gas company in the town of Villahermosa, Mexico. Even if a service provider interacts with government officials, the entity might not present much risk if its compensation is minimal or if the government officials are in low risk markets like Chile or Uruguay. On the other hand, if the third party is receiving significant funds, commonly interacts with officials on the company's behalf, operates in high-risk places, and/or operates in industries and sectors known for

THE FCPA IN LATIN AMERICA

corruption, then thorough due diligence and monitoring would be much more important.

Where the risk of foreign bribery is high and performing adequate due diligence is impossible, companies should not be afraid to walk away from doing business with those third parties, even if it means that the company will have to use a higher cost provider, or pass up a business opportunity. In the end, the additional costs or losses likely will be minimal compared to those associated with an FCPA enforcement action.

Handling Third-Party Due Diligence Backlogs

Many companies in Latin America are just now beginning to design, adopt, and implement third-party due diligence programs. Several factors are driving these recent developments, including the continued robust enforcement of the FCPA in the region and the adoption and enforcement of anti-corruption laws in local jurisdictions. In particular, the Brazilian government in March 2015 issued regulations for the Clean Companies Act that discuss compliance program expectations and emphasize third-party due diligence. The regulations go so far as to state that a company's anti-corruption compliance policies should apply not only to the company itself, but also to its third parties. Developments like these are driving companies to quickly improve their compliance work *vis a vis* their intermediaries.

Some companies in Latin America rely on literally thousands of third parties for their business, which creates a real practical challenge of how to vet them all. Even if a company has implemented procedures to vet new intermediaries going forward, it must still deal with the "backlog" of current vendors, a process commonly known as "remedial due diligence."

In 2011, for example, Switzerland-based Tyco International was doing business in Latin America, as well as other parts of the world, and reported that it had to design a due diligence program to address over 32,000 resellers, distributors, and other partners. In a 2011 survey conducted by Deloitte, 12% of the companies surveyed said they work with more than 10,000 business partners. If these companies spend just a few hundred dollars to review each third party, they would need to budget almost US$1 million just for basic due diligence. Even if they select just the top 10% as the highest risk and prioritize due diligence efforts on these companies first, they will still have a universe of hundreds of companies to vet in the first step. Although this may seem extreme, it may be necessary.

Below are some ways that companies can manage due diligence on their third-party backlogs:

> **Use the opportunity to build internal capacity.** Some companies see this situation as an opportunity to build the internal capabilities they eventually will need to run a fully functioning anti-corruption compliance program. For larger companies, comprehensive programs generally require numerous full-time staff with knowledge of how to navigate the complex and inevitable compliance issues that arise. Training qualified staff now will pave the way toward a streamlined compliance team in the future.

➤ **Outsource and negotiate a good rate.** If the company is large enough, it can outsource the work and use its leverage to negotiate a preferential rate. An overwhelming number of due diligence providers now make up the compliance space. Global companies can use this highly competitive landscape to their advantage.

➤ **Prioritize due diligence on the highest of the highest risk.** The company can roll out its due diligence in steps, first focusing on the highest of the highest risk. Which third parties assist the company in countries where corruption risk is most prevalent (*i.e.,* Argentina, Mexico, and Venezuela)? Which ones generate the most business? Which ones have known pending business? Which ones are paid on a commission basis? Which ones receive the most money from the company? After reviewing these entities, the company can then methodically work its way through the next levels of risk from there.

➤ **Prioritize due diligence where no contracts exist.** Companies can focus first on the business partners with whom they do not yet have a written contract in place. They can use the opportunity to establish contracts where they do not exist. Third parties in this group that are receiving the most money from the company can be reviewed first, and then others can be addressed from there. Contract formation and due diligence phases can thereby be wrapped together.

➤ **Build due diligence into contract renewals.** Companies can also look at the natural life cycles of the contracts currently in place to find opportunities to roll out due diligence. This helps minimize disruption of core business practices. Companies can also prioritize "evergreen" contracts, those in place for an indefinite period of time, since they will not be subject to a renewal process. Companies should also convert evergreen to term contracts as a basic risk mitigation step.

Transferring Third-Party Due Diligence to Business Units

One approach to managing third parties that is gaining steam among larger companies involves moving due diligence responsibilities from legal and compliance departments to business units. Putting commercial and sales teams in charge can address many common challenges. For one, it creates an efficient way of managing large numbers of third-party relationships. Relying on the chief compliance officer to vet all third parties can be impractical, so making the business units responsible for basic due diligence helps spread responsibility. It also frees up legal and compliance to focus on the more complex compliance issues.

Moreover, business personnel are often the closest to the third parties, making them better positioned to obtain information about the entity and walk it through the review. Business units also tend to take the process more seriously when they are required to "own it."

In addition, companies often find that they can reduce overall risks when business teams are put in charge, because business units often choose to use fewer third parties when they know doing so will involve issuing fewer questionnaires, signing fewer certifications, requesting audit rights in fewer contracts, and taking other precautions in fewer instances. They think twice about new relationships when they are forced to make the business case for them. For example, Siemens reduced its sales agents from 2,600 to 1,700 after conducting a compliance review in 2007. Of the 900 that were dropped, only 20 were due to compliance concerns. The rest were simply not needed, and they unnecessarily increased FCPA risks.

Relying on business units to conduct due diligence comes with potential downsides. In Latin America, for example, it is common to confront the dynamic of *compadrazgo*, a difficult-to-translate term describing the loyalty and trustworthiness that can develop between a company's employee and the outside representative. It is the type of relationship that can generate a productive work dynamic. But it can also facilitate corruption schemes when the participants become more loyal to each other than to their respective companies. This opens the door to the misdirection of company funds for illicit uses. In such situations, putting the business person in charge of diligence would only serve to compound the risk. Even if the business person is not directly involved in wrongdoing, he or she might be reluctant to conduct meaningful reviews, meaning that the possibility of indirect bribes would remain high.

Companies can address these risks in the following ways:

> **Implement procedures**. Companies can establish clear and easy-to-follow procedures for vetting their third parties, such as categorizing third parties based on risk and outline the required steps of review for each category. Standardized forms for questionnaires, certifications, and contract clauses make

program implementation more straightforward and consistent. The more automated the processes, the better.

> **Train and provide guidance.** Companies can use FCPA compliance trainings to ensure that business units understand common red flags that arise when dealing with third parties. Business teams should feel comfortable seeking guidance from compliance and legal departments on due diligence matters. If a third party is pushing back on audit rights, the legal department can intervene. If a flag is "pink" but not yet "red," the compliance department can offer input. Business units need to know that they have support at every step.

> **Conduct regular audits.** If business units know that their third-party due diligence efforts will be audited, they will be more likely to take them seriously.

Managing Third Parties Related To Government Officials

Oftentimes in Latin America, a company will find itself contracting with a third party that is owned or run by a government official or a relative of a government official, or that has a government official employed on staff. For example, in Central America, where business and government sectors are close knit, a company might wish to hire a law firm in which a legislator serves as a partner. In Andean countries with large indigenous communities, a company might want to contract an individual who happens to be a local community leader to provide services to it.

These situations can create FCPA compliance issues. For example, in 2002, the SEC fined BellSouth for FCPA violations after the company hired the wife of a Nicaraguan legislator to lobby the Nicaraguan Assembly to repeal a law restricting foreign ownership and paid her US$60,000 when her husband chaired the legislative committee overseeing the matter. At a minimum, these relationships will likely receive heightened scrutiny from FCPA enforcement officials, and thus companies should handle them with care. The risk is that payments companies make to these third parties might be interpreted as a means of providing a financial benefit to the official to obtain or retain a business benefit.

To manage situations like these, the key is to structure the relationship in a way that clearly establishes that the company is not paying the official to take an action in his or her own capacity as a public official, or to use his or her influence as a public official to influence another public official, to benefit the company. In essence, companies will want to demonstrate that they are not hiring the third party with corrupt intent.

To establish this, companies should take certain precautionary measures. The level of safeguards will depend on the circumstances. But companies will want to consider, and clearly document, answers to the following questions:

> **Is there a *bona fide* commercial reason to use the third party?** Does it have expertise in the area in which the company needs

assistance? Does it have a good reputation in the market for this type of work?

> **Does the compensation arrangement make sense in the market?** Is compensation reasonable given the work performed? Is it generally in sync with the fees that other firms charge? Are means of payment straightforward? Fees should be paid to the third party itself and never to the official. The company might even want to seek assurances from the third party that the official will not personally benefit from the engagement—that the fees will not be passed through to that individual, for example.

> **Does the official perform a role for the government that can directly benefit the company?** For there to be an FCPA violation, the company's payments must be made to influence an official act or decision by the official, to induce an official act or omission of the official in violation of a lawful duty, or to induce the official to influence a government act or decision. The company therefore might want to obtain a specific representation from the official that s/he will recuse him or herself from any government decisions that might affect the company and that s/he will not use special influence within the government to benefit the company. The more specific and comprehensive the representation, the better. Is the official in a position to represent the company before the government? Is the official in a position to initiate meetings with other officials about the company's business? Is the official in a position to appoint, promote, or compensate officials who can affect the company's business? Such scenarios should be considered, addressed, and avoided.

➤ **Does the contract make appropriate FCPA representations?** The contract with the third party should reference the FCPA issues at play. It can specify that the official will not be involved in any representation of or services to the company, or, if involved, will not personally receive payments directly or indirectly from the company. The third party can represent that it understands the FCPA's provisions and can certify that it will comply.

➤ **Has the company disclosed the relationship to the government?** Transparency is one of the best protections. The company can tell relevant government entities with which it interacts that it has retained the third party, that the official owns or works for the third party, and that the third party will be benefiting financially from the engagement. Steps like this can help minimize the possibility that the official would try to use his or her influence in the government to benefit personally.

Given the sensitivities of these engagements, companies should ensure they document all such compliance steps. They should conduct proper due diligence on the third party. They should also make sure that engaging the third party is legal under local law, even if the third party is affiliated with a government official.

Responding in the Face of Third-Party Corruption

More jurisdictions are now enforcing their anti-corruption laws in Latin America, and more companies are being caught up in bribery cases. As a result, it is not uncommon for some companies, especially large ones with thousands of third-party relationships, to confront situations in which they learn that a supplier, agent, or other business partner has been accused of corruption.

For example, the current investigation of Petrobras and its various contractors from the construction, financial, and other sectors by Brazilian and U.S. authorities has implicated numerous companies and agents. With each new entity named, other companies doing business in Brazil have found themselves wondering if their business, too, has been affected by allegations of misconduct.

Enforcement officials' basic expectation is that companies will undertake ongoing monitoring of business partners and third-party relationships. Monitoring helps companies identify when third-party integrity issues arise after the relationship has begun. Monitoring usually involves updating due diligence periodically, exercising audit rights, conducting periodic training, or requesting annual certifications by the entity. Monitoring should be risk-based and applied consistently.

Accusations alone do not equate to a third party's proven guilt, but they do require companies to respond appropriately. Usually, this means exercising audit rights within an agreement. These rights allow compliance teams to respond to reports of third parties' corrupt acts by taking a "kick the tires" approach. This might involve employing various measures, including:

> Reviewing agreements in place with the third party to make sure appropriate compliance language is included. If language is not there, the parties can determine how and when it can be incorporated, perhaps when the agreement is up next for renewal.

> Speaking with the business personnel who manage the relationship to understand the foreign corruption risks associated with the relationship. Does the third party interact with foreign officials on the company's behalf? Does it use other intermediaries to do so?

> Speaking with business personnel to obtain a sense of whether other red flags are present in the relationship. Has the third party been complying with the provisions of its agreement with the company? How is it being compensated for its work? Are services and costs well defined in the agreement?

> Requesting information about the third party's anti-corruption compliance program, especially when foreign bribery risks are at play.

Accusations that a third party has engaged in corrupt acts do not automatically mean that a company must cease all business activities with that entity, particularly when the reports of corruption involve a completely different country or business unit. Moreover, the fact that the entity might now be subject to an enforcement action probably means that it will start embracing robust compliance practices. Such enhanced compliance measures would mean that a company's business relationship with that entity may become more secure and less risky.

At the same time, knowledge of third party's wrongdoing should cause a company to take proactive measures to ensure that similar risks do not extend to its own operations. As always, all such compliance steps should be properly tracked and recorded.

Chapter 8

FCPA Enforcement in Latin America: Caught in the Web

Anti-corruption compliance is only half of the FCPA equation. Companies and individuals must also know what to do when confronting anti-corruption enforcement issues. For Latin American companies and businesspeople, the starting point is to understand how they can be subject to enforcement of a U.S. law by U.S. authorities. After that, it is important to know how to respond to enforcement efforts when they arise. This includes managing government inquiries, conducting internal investigations, and weighing voluntary disclosure of findings of wrongdoing to the authorities.

The Broad Reach of the FCPA into Latin America

The extraterritorial reach of the FCPA can be hard for foreign executives to grasp, and many might not realize they can face sanctions under U.S. anti-corruption laws.

Case studies, particularly regional examples, provide compelling evidence. The FCPA investigation of Brazil's Petrobras and Embraer, the 2013 arrest in the United States of the vice president of finance at Venezuela's Banco de Desarrollo Económico y Social for FCPA-related violations, and the SEC's fine of the CEO of LAN Airlines in 2016 are prime examples.

Below are five ways in which U.S. authorities can assert jurisdiction over non-U.S. companies and individuals under the FCPA's anti-bribery provisions:

1. **Issuers (15 U.S.C.§ 78dd-1).** The FCPA applies to Latin American companies with securities listed on a national securities exchange in the United States. These "issuers" are prohibited from making corrupt payments to non-U.S. officials, no matter where the payments occur in the world. This provision also applies to officers, directors, employees, and agents of issuers, even if they are Latin American. In addition to the FCPA's anti-bribery provisions, issuers are directly subject to the FCPA's accounting provisions, which require they maintain accurate books and records and internal controls.

2. **Domestic concerns (15 U.S.C. § 78dd-2).** Any individual who is a citizen or national of the United States, including any

corporation with its principal place of business in the United States, is known as a "domestic concern" and is subject to the FCPA no matter where it is operating in the world. This effectively means that Latin Americans with dual citizenship, or companies operating in the region with headquarters in the United States, can be subject under this provision.

3. **Territorial jurisdiction (15 U.S.C. § 78dd-3).** The FCPA prohibits any individual or company not covered by Sections 78dd-1 or 78dd-2, including those from Latin America, from performing any act in furtherance of bribery "while in the territory of the United States." This covers companies and officers, directors, employees, agents, and stockholders acting on behalf of their companies. The type of activity prohibited under Section 78dd-3 includes conducting meetings in the United States to plan bribery schemes, using U.S. bank accounts for such schemes, or sending e-mails from the United States authorizing bribe payments. In some circumstances, authorities have expanded the scope of this provision to hold defendants liable for causing an act to occur in the United States, such as sending mail to the United States or making phone calls into the United States that are connected to bribery, although in recent years, some courts have held against this more expansive application.

4. **Third-party agents.** Since the language of Sections 78dd-1, 78dd-2, and 78dd-3 includes actions by "agents" of covered entities, authorities in some instances have established jurisdiction over non-U.S. entities controlled by covered entities, such as non-U.S. subsidiaries, for their improper payments. However, at least one federal court has rejected

this interpretation as inconsistent with the FCPA's legislative history. For example, in *Dooley v. United Technologies Corp.*, 803 F. Supp. 428 (D.D.C. 1992), the U.S. District Court for the District of Columbia held that a British subsidiary of an American parent was not subject to the FCPA. The court began its analysis with the premise that statutes apply only within the territorial jurisdiction of the United States, unless Congress's contrary intent is clear. The only statutory language that could show such intent appeared in Section 78dd-2(g)(2)(B), which applied penalties to "any employee or agent of a domestic concern who is… otherwise subject to the jurisdiction of the United States." Congressional Conference Reports on this language make clear that the Conference intended the provision to apply to natural persons who happened to find themselves within the jurisdiction of the United States, but also that the Conference "recognized the inherent jurisdictional, enforcement, and diplomatic difficulties raised by the inclusion of foreign subsidiaries of U.S. companies in the direct prohibitions of the bill." Therefore, the court found that Congressional intent to apply the FCPA to subsidiaries outside the territorial jurisdiction of the United States was not clear and should not be read into the law. Of note, however, *Dooley* is a district court decision and is not binding in other federal jurisdictions. Thus, other courts could decide this issue differently.

5. **Conspiracy and aiding and abetting (18 U.S.C. §§ 2 and 371).** Perhaps the most likely way a Latin American company not publicly listed in the United States, and its personnel, can be subject to the FCPA is *indirectly* through federal conspiracy and aiding and abetting statutes. Under these theories,

individuals and companies that assist in the commission of an FCPA violation are considered "as guilty as if they had directly committed the offense themselves," as described in the FCPA Resource Guide. For example, when two or more people conspire to commit an offense against the United States, and at least one is an issuer, a domestic concern, or commits at least one reasonably overt act within the United States, U.S. authorities can assert jurisdiction over all conspirators. Similarly, any individual or company that aids and abets a violation can be subject to jurisdiction without taking any act in furtherance of the violation within the United States. To assert aiding and abetting, the U.S. government must prove that an independent FCPA violation was committed by the principal actor. Conspiracy theories, in particular, are often asserted by U.S. prosecutors. Courts trying these cases have allowed prosecutors to bring in evidence that might otherwise be difficult to admit and to avoid substantial jurisdictional challenges that might otherwise make it difficult to charge a foreigner with a criminal act. Use of the conspiracy theories also helps prosecutors tell compelling stories of corruption schemes involving multiple actors. These charges are not without limits, however. In 2015, one federal court limited this form of jurisdictional reach by requiring that authorities also establish that the non-U.S. entity was an agent of a covered entity.

How FCPA Enforcement Officials Discover Violations

People in Latin America often wonder how FCPA enforcement officials discover violations in the first place. Bribery by its very nature plays out in the darkness, and foreign bribery usually happens far away from the United States. Those committed to making improper payments are also committed to making sure their tracks are covered. So the chances that the DOJ or the SEC would learn about a violation normally would seem slim.

In reality, foreign bribery can come to light in many ways. The following are some examples:

> **Voluntary disclosures**. The U.S. government encourages companies to self-disclose the violations they uncover. As the FCPA Resource Guide states: "The DOJ and SEC place a high premium on self-reporting, along with cooperation and remedial efforts, in determining the appropriate resolution of FCPA matters." These efforts can lead to fine reductions under §8C2.5(g) of the U.S. Sentencing Guidelines by decreasing a company's culpability score. For example, in BizJet's deferred prosecution agreement, the DOJ noted the company's "extraordinary" cooperation including self-disclosure, an extensive internal investigatio ...aking U.S. and foreign employees available for interviews, collecting "voluminous" evidence, and extensive remediation. Accordingly, BizJet paid a monetary penalty of only US$11.8 million—30% less than the minimum of the US$17 million to US$34 million fine

range recommended by the Sentencing Guidelines. It is worth noting that despite such examples, some FCPA practitioners believe that the benefits of self-disclosure are not always clear and can be hard to quantify. Companies continue to self-disclose violations, nonetheless, and will likely continue to do so. Thus, they remain a source of information to the government.

> **Whistleblower tips.** The U.S. Dodd-Frank Act (15 U.S.C. § 78u-6) has changed the enforcement landscape by creating whistleblower incentives and protections. According to the SEC's Office of the Whistleblower report, whistleblower tips regularly expose corporate foreign bribery. Tips from Latin America are considerable. In fiscal year 2014, the SEC received 50 tips from 10 countries in the region. In fiscal year 2015, it received 48 tips from 12 countries. It is not clear whether these tips relate to the FCPA specifically or other securities issues as well. Whistleblowers have many different reasons for coming forward, but the most important incentive is financial, since tipsters can receive up to 30% of any fine recovered by the government.

> **Press reports.** Reporters are aggressive, and sensational bribery stories sell papers, especially in Latin America. For example, some in Mexico say that the country's 2015 reform of anti-corruption laws, which has ushered in a new National Anti-Corruption System, was fueled largely by a relentless press. Local media consistently reported on signs that President Peña Nieto's wife and his finance minister received preferential support from a company by buying houses in return for channeling government contracts to that company. The National Water Commission minister was reported

to have used a government helicopter for personal matters. Media pursued stories on how local authorities and police colluded with a drug cartel in the state of Guerrero, resulting in the disappearance of 43 students there. Such an active press serves to expose illicit schemes, and FCPA enforcement officials read news reports from around the world. An aggressive press, in combination with an aggressive FCPA enforcement environment, creates the perfect storm to help expose FCPA violations.

> **Competitors.** An easy way for a company to complicate a competitor's business pursuits is to bring its competitor's shady acts to enforcement officials' attention. Companies in the same industry are often well positioned to discover their competition's wrongdoing. For example, if one company is asked to pay a bribe to a government official in exchange for a permit, refuses to pay, and then sees a competitor quickly receive the same permit from the same official, it is a sign that the competitor paid the bribe. Similarly if a company is wrongly disqualified in a public procurement while its higher priced competitor wins the contract, it may be evidence of corruption at play. It only takes an anonymous e-mail to the DOJ or SEC to expose such potential wrongdoing.

> **Industry sweeps.** The DOJ and the SEC often take an industry-by-industry, sector-by-sector approach to enforcing the FCPA, which offers unique ways of uncovering wrongdoing. By investigating one company in an industry, for example, the government might learn of other companies that are using the same corrupt agent or consultant, particularly where other companies are generating significant business from a foreign

government entity known for corruption. Such leads often help uncover additional violations, akin to the events that are unfolding in the investigation of Petrobras and the numerous construction companies that have been implicated.

> **Disgruntled employees.** An employee who is terminated or is otherwise upset with his employer and who knows of wrongdoing at the company might have a strong incentive to disclose such information to the government.

> **The Federal Bureau of Investigation ("the FBI").** In March 2015, the FBI created a dedicated anti-corruption unit. With 23 agents devoted specifically to anti-corruption enforcement, this unit travels internationally to assist with investigations and work with local law enforcement on bribery cases. Agents are positioned to uncover evidence of wrongdoing not formerly known by FCPA enforcement officials.

The Importance of Internal FCPA Investigations

For companies that have managed FCPA compliance for years, the importance of investigating allegations of internal wrongdoing might seem obvious. When an indication of an improper payment arises, it is better to learn the truth than to ignore it or to assume an innocent explanation that may not be supported by the facts. Indeed, FCPA enforcement officials explicitly expect companies to determine what actually happened. The FCPA Resource Guide states, "[O]nce an allegation is made, companies should have in place an efficient, reliable, and properly funded process for investigating the allegation and documenting the company's response, including any disciplinary or remediation measures taken."

But for a Latin American company just beginning to implement anti-corruption compliance controls, the value of investigating itself might not necessarily be self-evident. For one, internal investigations can be costly, and the business justification might not be readily apparent. Moreover, some Latin American companies may believe they should not do the government's job, and that if law enforcement authorities want to learn about a potential violation of law, the burden should be on them to build their case. Relatedly, in many Latin American jurisdictions, the concepts of cooperation and plea bargaining are not well-developed, and it seems far-fetched that a company would admit a violation to prosecutors before a case begins.

Despite these considerations, conducting an internal investigation, either before or after the government learns about an issue, can be crucial to protecting a company's own interests for multiple reasons.

By being ahead of a government investigation, companies can realize the following benefits:

> **Adequately resolving the problem.** If a company has a bribery problem, it can only fix it if it knows the facts. Without understanding the full scope of the issue—such as the people and business units involved, the extent of funds at stake, and how high the problem goes in the organization—it is difficult

to adequately address. Wrongdoers can only be disciplined if a company can identify them. Controls weaknesses can only be remediated if a company understands them.

➢ **Preventing bigger problems.** When a company ignores a problem, it likely will become worse, not better. Bribery has a way of growing; bribe requests become larger, and business becomes more dependent on shortcuts. Hidden accounts initially designed to transfer funds to public officials might be put to use to transfer money back to employees themselves. Allowing a problem to fester can have a broader effect of encouraging more bad actors within an organization. When one employee sees a colleague get away with misconduct, he or she might be more inclined to violate policy, too.

➢ **Avoiding bad business.** Ignoring a bribery allegation can have negative effects on business. Bribery often goes hand in hand with management issues; people who are not effective managers sometimes use shortcuts to ensure effective performance. Since companies base their investment decisions on performance, they will want to know the basis of performance, including when it is based on unsustainable conduct.

➢ **Meeting disclosure obligations.** Publicly listed companies need to be aware of material developments to comply with disclosure requirements. If a company is not following up on allegations raised, it is difficult to be fully confident that it is giving the market accurate information. There might be a large contingent liability that it does not yet understand. In this way, disclosure obligations can have the effect of compelling companies to conduct internal investigations in situations where they might not otherwise have done so.

➤ **Preparing for a potential inquiry.** Simply because a company is not yet aware of any law enforcement investigation into its conduct does not mean it is not occurring. An employee, a vendor, or some other third party may already have reported an issue to authorities and they may already be investigating the matter, and intentionally not alerting the company to the existence of the investigation. If authorities do confront the company with an investigation, the company will be in a markedly better position to respond, having already conducted its own investigation into the matter.

Furthermore, an internal investigation is much easier for a company if it can be conducted before the government becomes involved. After a company becomes a target in a government review, it can be subject to seizure of documents, grand jury inquiries, and other unpleasant realities of formal criminal investigations.

Even when the government has commenced its own investigation before a company fully understands the issues, the company still will want to conduct its own parallel internal investigation for two important reasons. First, it helps the company control its message. When a company develops and a̶ ̶ses the facts itself, it is better positioned to control how facts are interpreted and presented to both the government and the public. For example, while a prosecutor might look at a narrow set of facts suggesting egregious wrongdoing, a company may be able to show that the conduct was isolated or limited to low-level employees. While one bad e-mail could significantly shift a prosecutor's interest in a case, a company might be able to explain that the context of that one e-mail to demonstrate that is not actually incriminating, or how the company has already disciplined the employee who engaged in the conduct. By failing to investigate an issue, a company runs the risk of ceding control to prosecutors. By not proactively correcting failures that might eventually become public, a company could find itself scrambling to respond to bad press.

Secondly, conducting an internal investigation helps protect its results from outside scrutiny because it may be covered by privilege protections. Internal investigations led by lawyers allow companies to establish attorney-client privilege over material related to the investigation, at least in the United States. Learning the facts and assessing the company's exposure in a privileged way gives a company greater control and options that it might not otherwise have when responding to government inquiries. Protecting information is also extremely important given the potential for follow-on civil litigation that may occur. An eventual plaintiff could seek to discover company information and statements made to the government. One bad e-mail in the hands of a zealous plaintiff can significantly raise a company's own settlement calculation.

When companies consider these various components, they begin to realize that not addressing an indication of wrongdoing, and managing it appropriately, can have serious consequences, in terms of costs, reputation, and liability. Internal investigations can sometimes be expensive, but they can also, in the long run, result in cost savings that include lower fines, less chance of larger civil judgments, protected reputation, and sustainable business practices.

When to Use Outside Counsel for FCPA Investigations

More and more companies in Latin America are developing internal resources to manage potential FCPA violations. They bring to bear triage committees, internal audit teams, investigation units, and in-house lawyers when running issues to ground. Given these trends, companies must increasingly consider when to rely on outside legal counsel, including lawyers from the United States, for FCPA investigations.

To decide this issue, it is important to consider various questions:

> **Is the investigation record likely to be reviewed by others?** One of the main reasons to hire outside counsel is credibility. Investigations by inside counsel are subject to suspicion as biased—or, worse, as being whitewashed. Outside counsel bring, or should bring, both independence and expertise to the table. If the record of investigation could end up on the desk of a DOJ attorney, a company will want it to be as credible as possible. Thus, it is important to consider whether a potential whistleblower, disgruntled employee, or aggressive journalist might bring the issue to light.

> **What is the company's reputation?** Jeffrey Knox, the former chief of the DOJ's Criminal Fraud Section, stated, "I think credibility and reputation go a long way with us . . . A lot does have to do I think with the reputation of the company and the counsel and even to some extent the outside law firm." Certain

companies with leading compliance practices, like GE and Siemens, have built strong reputations. Their internal reviews will inevitably carry more weight. Others that are unknown, especially companies based in Latin America that have yet to build a track record with U.S. or local authorities, might not have the same automatic credibility.

➤ **What are the company's internal capabilities?** Investigations are often complex because foreign bribery schemes tend to touch multiple jurisdictions, actors, and cultures. Companies must consider whether they have the staffing to handle the matter. Companies might ask, do their personnel have local language skills, expertise in local laws, and the manpower to handle complicated reviews? By relying on internal resources, will individuals get pulled away from their normal duties? If the answers are yes, companies are more likely to look externally for help.

➤ **How severe are the allegations?** Many companies tend to start reviews internally and assess whether outside legal assistance is necessary as they go. For example, they will seek outside assistance as soon as information collected indicates violations of law rather than merely violations of internal policy. They will look outside when evidence implicates the involvement of high-level executives, or when problems are systemic, rather than isolated.

➤ **How credible are the allegations?** Whistleblower allegations are credible when tips are corroborated by evidence, or the person making the report has direct knowledge of the wrongdoing. Both circumstances suggest that companies should use outside counsel. When tips appear baseless, on the other hand, internal reviews tend to be more appropriate.

These determinations are rarely easy to make and involve numerous factors. Companies that have already made significant investments in their compliance programs generally come out on the issue in one of two ways. They have built impressive internal capabilities for foreign bribery matters and can field many issues themselves. They also recognize that, at times, reliance on qualified counsel is essential. As one former compliance officer said: "When a company makes significant investments to build a robust compliance program, it shortchanges itself by attempting to go the last mile on the cheap."

Knowing When to Voluntarily Disclose

Neither a company nor its directors or officers have an affirmative obligation under the FCPA to disclose knowledge of a violation. But enforcement officials stress that there are benefits to doing so, including more lenient treatment and credit when penalties are calculated. Former DOJ Fraud Section Chief Jeffrey Knox said, "[C]ompanies that self-disclose conduct are in a much better position than those who don't. They are much more likely to be given deference by us than those that are receiving a phone call from us telling them about the conduct." James Cole, former Deputy Attorney General of the United States, dedicated much time to talking about self-disclosures of FCPA violations. "We at the Department are committed to demonstrating the benefits to your working cooperatively with us," he said in 2013 while at the DOJ. "We want to work with you and we will continue our efforts to provide tangible benefits to reward you for doing so."

Jason Jones, the former Assistant Chief of the DOJ's FCPA unit, has said that companies that choose not to disclose are taking a calculated risk that enforcement will find out. He calls this a "gamble," since a whistleblower, a wiretap, a foreign government, another government agency, or a competitor could all be sources of disclosing the matter. He also says that the downsides to not disclosing are real: "The odds are we are going to make it hurt a little bit."

Companies should consider the following issues when facing the question of disclosure:

➤ **How egregious was the violation?** Did the misconduct involve high-ranking employees? Was it extensive and systemic in the organization? The better the facts, the more inclined authorities will be to extend significant leniency to the company. The worse the facts, the less beneficial treatment a company might expect. There are certainly instances where disclosure could lead to lenient treatment, even when facts are bad. But the question concerning the egregiousness of the violation is still relevant to the overall picture.

➤ **Does the company have a good story to tell?** Was the issue discovered through its internal controls? Did the company quickly respond to the misconduct and discipline wrongdoers? Was the issue an exception to an otherwise strong compliance framework? The more the company can tell a story showing that management tried to prevent corruption risks, the better it will look in the disclosure context.

> **Is the company ready for a protracted and uncertain negotiation with the government?** By self-disclosing, a company helps position itself to drive the internal review, remediation process, and framing of issues for the government, but it also close to guarantees itself a lengthy, involved process of discussions and negotiations with authorities. This means more legal fees and potential disruption of business operations. The government might even request that the investigation be broadened. Even with credit for disclosure and cooperation, the matter could end with significant penalties and sanctions.

> **How likely is the issue to come to the attention of FCPA enforcement authorities?** Could there be a whistleblower? Is another company involved in the wrongdoing likely to disclose? Might a competitor bring the issue to the government's attention? Is the press likely to uncover the facts? The more likely the misconduct is to come to light, the more important it will be to bring it to the government's attention first.

> **Do individuals have exposure?** FCPA enforcers are much more focused today on holding individuals accountable for FCPA misconduct. This means that, if a company discloses an issue, it should expect the government to consider actions against responsible individuals themselves. This might affect disclosure calculations, especially for smaller companies.

> **What are the reputation risks at play?** Considerations of the company's reputation can cut in two directions. Some companies might be less inclined to disclose for fear of negative

publicity. Others might see disclosure as a helpful way of controlling public perceptions.

➤ **Would other enforcement authorities have an interest?** If the misconduct involves several jurisdictions, the company could expect other authorities to pick up the case. The sanctions programs of the World Bank and other multilateral development banks could be triggered. Before revealing the issue to the U.S. government, companies should consider the broader implications.

Disclosure has led to tangible benefits for numerous companies. For example, in 2013 Ralph Lauren Corporation became the first company to ever negotiate double non-prosecution agreements with the SEC and the DOJ. Although Ralph Lauren's subsidiary bribed multiple Argentine customs officials repeatedly over a period of five years, both agencies noted the company's self-disclosure, cooperation, and remedial measures. Accordingly, the company's combined penalties were only US$1.6 million. Similarly, BizJet's settlement for US$11.8 million represented a 30% reduction off the minimum suggested fine of US$17.1 million under the Sentencing Guidelines, given its self-disclosure and what the DOJ called "extraordinary cooperation, including conducting an extensive internal investigation, voluntarily making U.S. and foreign employees available for interviews, and collecting, analyzing and organizing voluminous evidence and information for the department."

Why FCPA Investigations Are Costly

FCPA investigation costs can easily regularly climb into the millions of dollars. While Stryker paid just over US$13 million in its settlement with U.S. authorities that covered transactions in Argentina and Mexico, for example, it also spent a reported US$75 million on its investigation. In another example, Avon reportedly spent more than US$350 million on its investigation covering Argentina, Brazil, and Mexico, among other countries, while Willbros reportedly spent more than US$10 million on an investigation that involved Ecuador and Nigeria.

FCPA investigations can be expensive for several reasons, including:

> **The scope of the misconduct**. When a company conducts an internal investigation, it usually will focus on the country or countries implicated in the initial allegations. After it vets those issues, it is not uncommon for authorities to ask the following series of questions: How do you know the issues do not exist elsewhere in the company's operations throughout the world? How do you know that the problem is isolated and not systemic? All of a sudden, a limited investigation becomes full blown.

> **The length of the investigation**. Embraer received its subpoena from the SEC in 2010 and the investigation continued as of mid-2016. Avon started its investigation in June 2008 and resolved the FCPA action in December 2014, more than six years later. These timeframes are not abnormal. Internal

investigations are rarely quick. Even after the company collects and analyzes the facts, it still may have to negotiate a resolution with authorities if FCPA violations did occur. Each step usually comes with more costs, costs on lawyers, investigators, forensic accountants, computer analysts, and all of the other types of service providers needed to conduct and settle a government investigation.

➢ **The scope of the review and interviews.** When presented with an allegation of foreign bribery, the U.S. government will often ask a company to conduct a thorough internal investigation, if it has not already started one. The time and effort needed to do this is significant. Each company unit and individual implicated in a scheme can trigger its own set of interviews and document review. The more people involved, the more document and e-mail senders, recipients, and custodians will have to be included in a computer forensic search. Companies often will use outside resources to perform many of these tasks to ensure that the investigation is credible and independent, generally more expensive than relying on in-house resources. One startling example is the Siemens investigation, which ended in the most expensive FCPA settlement to date. Siemens reported that its investigation cost the company an estimated US$1 billion and included roughly 1,750 interviews, over 1,000 informational briefings, 82 million documents electronically searched and 14 million documents reviewed, 38 million financial transactions analyzed, and 10 million bank records reviewed.

➢ **The geographic scope of the investigation.** Increasingly companies have to interact with enforcement authorities in a number of countries. For example, Brazilian authorities initiated their investigation of Embraer after the DOJ and the SEC had commenced their investigations. Multi-jurisdictional investigations require companies to hire additional outside lawyers in multiple countries and make additional efforts to ensure that activity in numerous jurisdictions has been reviewed. Adding to the difficulty is the fact that countries in the region have varying characteristics that can affect investigations, meaning that investigators cannot take uniform approaches region-wide. For example, the meanings of words might vary by country even when they are in Spanish. When discussing business contracts in Mexico, the word *cancelar* means "to cancel;" in Paraguay it means "to pay,"—completely different meanings. The Spanish in Argentina is not the same as the Spanish in Venezuela.

➢ **The degree of personal liability**. When the government investigates company employees, the company often pays the individuals' legal fees, resulting in additional expenses. The non-monetary costs associated with these investigations are equally detrimental to a company, in that they create a significant burden on upper management and distract comply leadership from its normal responsibilities.

Taking these costs into consideration, modest investments in robust anti-corruption compliance programs up front begin to make more economic sense. For one, with an effective program in place, wrongdoing is often identified before it causes too much damage. If an internal investigation is necessary, its scope is generally is likely to be smaller. With a compliance infrastructure already in place, a company can more effectively determine the extent of wrongdoing without a full-blown review. It can look to its regular compliance audit reports to get a sense of how many countries or divisions might be implicated. It can rely on records of third-party due diligence and monitoring, and training of company officials and vetting of business partners, to help isolate activity under review. Without a compliance program in place, however, a company risks the alternative: the potential for a widespread investigation.

Minimizing Internal Investigation Costs

Given the high stakes of internal investigations, companies have built-in motivations to pay whatever is needed to reach credible findings. A faulty investigation can leave a company not only exposed, but also faced with additional penalties.

However, companies can be smart about the money they spend on these reviews in the following ways:

> **Up-front preparation.** One of the most expensive elements of an internal investigation is compensating practitioners for the time spent "in country." Costs for transportation, accommodations, and meals, as well as the billable hours accumulated when investigators are on-the-clock, add up. To minimize these costs, up-front preparation is essential. Investigators should gain access beforehand to as many relevant documents as possible, understand the landscape, key players, and organizational structures of the units being investigated, and

consider interviewing by phone relevant witnesses or employees when such "long-distance" interviews would not be prejudicial to the investigation. Preliminary preparation also helps rule out some issues and increases focus on others, which can streamline "in-country" work.

➤ **Doubling up.** It is not uncommon for highly specialized FCPA legal and investigative firms to have several matters going on at once in a particular country or region. This creates the potential for economies of scale that can reduce costs to each client. Transportation to the region and other costs can be spread among various clients, leading to substantial savings.

➤ **Using language experts.** Language translations of documents during an investigation can be expensive. Such costs are minimized with the use of multilingu .wyers and investigators who can review all documents, relevant and irrelevant, without incurring translation fees. Then, companies will only need to purchase official translations of the most relevant and sensitive documents.

➤ **Utilizing technology.** Technology can drive down costs. Database services help accelerate large-scale document reviews. Skype helps facilitate communication.

➤ **Visas and shots**. Incidental costs associated with travel, like fees for visas and costs of doctor visits, vaccine shots, and malaria medication, can add up. Satisfying such requirements can also be time consuming, delaying an investigation when a client needs a quick resolution. The more often a practitioner does international work, the more likely it is that s/he will have the multi-year entry visa for the target country or the relevant vaccines already.

➢ **Cooperating, but not "rolling over."** When enforcement officials are advising a company to conduct a specific type of investigation, the most experienced FCPA practitioners know how to negotiate a reasonable plan. The instinct may be to do everything requested by the government. This can lead to costly and unnecessary investigative steps. The DOJ and the SEC often will consider proposed alternatives that are less costly and intrusive, but that still fulfill the objective of uncovering and remediating improper activity.

➢ **Knowing when to stop.** Tracking down every e-mail and interviewing every person tangentially involved with a matter under investigation might not be necessary. Experienced investigators will know when an issue has been adequately run to ground and findings substantially supported.

➢ **Allocating responsibilities.** Large-scale and complex investigations have the potential to involve numerous actors. Nothing is more frustrating to an internal compliance officer than an army of in-house counsel, outside lawyers, local foreign counsel, forensic accountants, investigators, and database technology experts with no clear allocation of roles and responsibilities. With no set plan, actors are likely to repeat the same work. Lack of communication thwarts effectiveness. This can result in unnecessary billable hours.

Establishing Credibility with FCPA Enforcement Officials

Executives of Latin American companies can find it hard to accept when they are under investigation for potential FCPA violations. When companies learn that liability may be civil and criminal, may involve both corporate and individual liability, and certainly implicates significant cost and reputational considerations, the effects can be overwhelming. In situations like these, it is imperative that companies engaging with enforcement officials establish and maintain credibility with them to achieve the best possible outcomes.

To do so, they should consider the following steps.

➤ **Have a plan**. From the beginning, enforcements agencies will want to know who at the company is calling the shots and who will be doing the actual work. Is the general counsel, chief compliance officer, or audit committee running the review? Is the investigation utilizing internal resources or external ones, or both? How is the company ensuring the investigation's independence? Companies should make sure they utilize only one point of contact with authorities.

➤ **Follow internal investigation best practices**. If a company has not already built credibility with enforcement officials, it will want to rely on outside counsel that has. Whatever the company does, it should be sure not to make novice errors. This means following investigative best practices like preserving evidence, conducting internal interviews with proper protocol, and defining scopes of review in ways that make sense, among other things. When an internal investigation is properly calibrated, the company is better positioned to respond to the inevitable questions of FCPA officials about the types of evidence collected and the individuals, business units, countries, and foreign officials implicated in the wrongdoing. If the company does not demonstrate seriousness, the government could quickly lose confidence in its ability to manage the issues, complicating a company's chances of obtaining a favorable resolution. More troublesome, it can mean that the government might choose to take a more active role in guiding, or even conducting, the investigation itself.

➤ **Move quickly.** Obstacles and logistical hurdles inevitably arise when mounting a response to an FCPA issue—such as the need to obtain travel visas, understand the types of investigative efforts permitted under local laws, and gather and assess initial facts. The longer a company waits to start, the more likely it is that evidence could be lost or that individuals with information could be unavailable. The company also risks allowing a corrupt scheme to continue. For these reasons, companies should move quickly to determine the facts and address the issues. Failing to do so would not look good in the eyes of the DOJ and the SEC.

➤ **Be polite, honest, and direct.** A company should not lose sight of the human element of its interactions with enforcement officials. If it decides it is in the best interest of the company to cooperate with the enforcement agency, it should do so in a way that allows it to obtain the fullest possible benefit of that cooperation. This means being prompt in responding to inquiries, producing translations of foreign language documents, highlighting the nature and substance of documents it produces, and explaining the reasons for delays of supplemental productions. When officials ask to interview company employees, the company should assist in producing those employees in a timely and cooperative way. Cooperation should be proactive, not passive. This means reaching out to officials to make sure their requests are being met, instead of merely waiting for their inquiries. It can also be helpful to take the time to point out important or significant documents or information, even when they might not be favorable to the company's position. As one colleague stated, "DOJ and SEC officials are smart people. They will figure this stuff out. So you might as well make it easier for them."

> **Strike the right balance between cooperation and advocacy.** Resolutions when FCPA violations have been discovered are specialized situations. Companies cannot be too pushy when they are trying to reach a settlement agreement. For example, they should be careful not to overly assert the attorney-client or work-product privileges and do so only in light of relevant standards. This means being conscious of the often non-attorney client privileged communications of in-house counsel. It means not confusing government investigations with regular civil litigation, with its occasional document production gamesmanship. Production of documents is none other than a further important step in a company's efforts to cooperate with an inquiry. At the same time, companies should not roll over. FCPA enforcement officials can be aggressive, and companies need to know when and how to push back. When they do so, their decisions should be educated and well-reasoned. This is often difficult to do well without the advice of

experienced FCPA counsel. Lawyers who regularly engage in discussions with the government are familiar with the nuances of the statute's application, knowing when it makes sense to concede to government requests, and when it is appropriate to refuse. Approaching resolution discussions in this way, companies are able to build credibility from a position of strength, even when taking positions contrary to the theories advocated by enforcement agencies.

— ◆ —

When it comes to anti-corruption enforcement matters, it is critical to remember that the FCPA is no longer the only anti-corruption law to consider in Latin America. Dramatic developments in local laws and enforcement trends in countries like Brazil, Mexico, Colombia, Guatemala, Chile, and others throughout the region mean that companies must carefully consider how to respond to government inquiries into potential wrongdoing. No matter the country or enforcement regime, it is essential for a company to learn the facts for itself related to the potential wrongdoing. Without knowledge of the facts, a company is left vulnerable to enforcement by U.S. authorities, local authorities in the region, or both. With that information, the company is positioned to calculate when it should seek leniency, how it might defend an unsubstantiated accusation, or the ways in which it can remediate internal controls weaknesses to prevent similar issues from occurring again in the future.

— ◆ —

This book began by making the point that companies and businesspeople now operate in a truly multi-lateral enforcement environment, where concepts of business ethics are no longer dictated by one set of authorities in the United States, where standards for compliant businesses are more regularly expected throughout the region. Pressures are being placed on U.S. and Latin American companies by local laws, investors, external auditors, and other stakeholders to elevate anti-corruption compliance as a core component of business. In many ways, these dynamics make a company's efforts to work in a compliant manner much easier. Companies no longer are forced to adopt and promote their compliance policies in a legal vacuum. This book is intended to provide guidance to companies embarking upon anti-corruption compliance efforts, no matter where they occur in the Latin American region.

Index

Argentina	7, 9, 10, 15, 16, 18, 23, 24, 25, 33, 34, 52, 56-59, 64, 86, 88, 92, 94, 95, 96, 105, 109, 114-115, 119, 124, 143, 148, 149, 156, 166, 170, 199, 200, 202
Attorney client privilege	193, 208
Audits, compliance	37, 89, 91, 92, 98, 111, 118-119, 121-123, 127, 145, 154, 173, 177
Bolivia	10, 30, 54, 105, 144, 150
Brazil	1, 5, 6, 7, 9, 10, 11-12, 14, 16, 18, 23, 25, 27, 31, 37, 39, 43, 51, 54, 59-62, 64, 65, 70, 84, 88, 92, 105, 109, 110, 112, 113, 117, 119, 120, 124, 131, 135, 142, 145, 148, 149, 165, 177, 182, 200, 202, 209
Brazil Clean Companies Act	11-12, 59, 168
Charitable donations / political contributions	62, 69, 75, 86, 93, 98, 122
Chile	7, 23-25, 63-66, 84, 157, 167, 182, 209

Colombia	5, 7, 9, 24, 25, 30, 54, 66-69, 84, 105, 110, 131, 141-142, 166, 209
Costa Rica	10, 27, 39, 54, 109, 111
Cuba	10, 30, 54
Culture	2, 14-17, 22-23, 46, 61-62, 131-145
Customs	17, 33-36, 57, 88, 148
Declinations	96, 98
Dominican Republic	10, 105
Due diligence, third party	32, 33, 47, 58, 61, 68, 79, 92, 98, 100, 107, 120, 129, 148, 150-179, 203
Due diligence, acquisition	45-47, 100, 106, 127, 135, 151
Ecuador	9, 10, 15, 54, 105, 156, 200
El Salvador	6, 54
Ernst and Young	45
Extortion / security payments	24, 36-38, 68, 71, 79
Facilitating payments	31, 42-44
FCPA Accounting Provisions	78, 78, 86-94, 97, 113-120, 182
FCPA Anti-Bribery Provisions	40, 42, 71, 85-86, 182
FCPA Resource Guide	98, 104, 107, 126, 156, 157, 185, 186, 189
Foreign official	25, 69, 77
Forensic accounting	114-120, 122, 123, 145
FTI Consulting	70, 124
Gifts, travel, entertainment and hospitality	29, 38-42, 44, 85, 90, 92-93, 98, 110, 123, 129, 154

Guatemala	10, 12, 14, 18, 105, 209
Haiti	24, 34, 76, 86, 104
Honduras	10, 105, 143
Internal investigations	3, 32, 79, 81, 84, 181, 189-196, 200-209
Internal reporting / hotlines	122, 142-145
Jurisdiction	13, 111, 182-185
Latin America Corruption Survey	7, 9, 27, 36, 62, 70, 76, 82, 108, 137, 150-151
Mexico	1, 2, 4, 7, 9, 12, 14, 15, 16, 23, 25, 27, 31, 32, 36, 37, 47, 54, 55, 70-73, 84, 85, 86, 93, 94, 99, 105, 106, 109, 110, 124, 131, 133, 135, 140, 141, 148, 149, 159, 166, 167, 170, 187, 200, 202, 209
Mintz Group	121-122
Nicaragua	10, 54, 92, 104, 174
OECD Anti-Bribery Convention	7, 11, 64, 67, 84
OECD Foreign Bribery Report	26, 85, 148, 159
Panama	10, 23, 27, 54, 166
Paraguay	6, 10, 23, 30, 54, 104, 144, 202
Peru	7, 9, 10, 30, 64, 65, 73-76, 84, 105, 124, 165, 166
PricewaterhouseCoopers	61, 115
Public procurement / government contracting	24, 26-30, 59, 61, 72, 75-76, 85, 105-106, 114, 188

Red flags	29, 32, 48, 89, 91, 92, 94, 111, 113, 117, 122, 147, 156, 160-164, 166, 173, 178
Regulatory risks	10, 25, 30-32, 52, 56, 61, 63, 67, 73, 77, 79, 86, 148, 159
Risk assessments	25-26, 105-106, 122, 129
State-owned enterprises	24, 27, 28, 38, 72, 77, 85, 105
Tone from the top	111, 138
Trace International	14, 107
Training	32, 35, 37, 46, 72, 89, 93-94, 98, 108-114, 125, 129, 133, 135, 138, 141, 153, 160, 169, 173, 177, 203
Transparency International Corruption Perceptions Index	8, 9, 10, 24, 53, 56, 63, 67, 70, 74, 76, 104
Uruguay	6, 24, 54, 156, 167
U.S. Federal Sentencing Guidelines	104, 125, 186-187, 199
Venezuela	12, 14, 18, 24-25, 30, 34, 36, 52, 54, 67, 70, 76-80, 89, 92, 94, 104, 111, 124, 143, 166, 170, 182, 202
Voluntary disclosures	181, 186-187, 196-199
Whistleblowers	96, 110, 187, 194, 195, 197, 198
World Bank	8, 29, 30, 31, 48, 56, 63, 66, 67, 70, 73, 74, 77, 199